NO MERE PASTIME

NO MERE PASTIME

A LIFE IN HIGH PLACES

KEN STANTON

Alive Book Publishing

No Mere Pastime
A Life in High Places
Copyright © 2021 by Ken Stanton

All rights reserved. No part of this book may be reproduced or transmitted in any form or by any means without written permission from the publisher and author.

Additional copies may be ordered from the publisher for educational, business, promotional or premium use. For information, contact ALIVE Book Publishing at: alivebookpublishing.com, or call (925) 837-7303.

Book and Cover Design by Alex P. Johnson
All photos are by the author unless cited otherwise.

ISBN 13
978-1-63132-133-7

Library of Congress Control Number: 2021909537

Library of Congress Cataloging-in-Publication Data
is available upon request.

First Edition

Published in the United States of America by ALIVE Book Publishing
an imprints of Advanced Publishing LLC
3200 A Danville Blvd., Suite 204, Alamo, California 94507
alivebookpublishing.com

PRINTED IN THE UNITED STATES OF AMERICA

10 9 8 7 6 5 4 3 2 1

Acknowledgments

No Mere Pastime is a deeply personal book sourced mainly from memory and journals. Yet there are many people whose help, knowingly or unknowingly were key to its success. I'd like to thank the many climbing partners and friends who have shared a rope over the decades: Brian Estes, Bruce Hope, Forrest Shute, Wade Mills, Warren Egbert, Jeanna Atkins, Curt Dixon, Jeff Sutcliffe, Murray Sims, Burt Geller, Mark Hrubant, Greg Gollan, Jack Fisher, Joannie Harris Stoneberg, Tom Smith and Krista Smith, Shelley Presson, Susan Schaeffer, Robin Madgwick, Steve Zanelli, Mike Buckley, Sylvie Baroux, Jim Lundine, Bruce Bailey, Scott Fields, Reg Jennings, Father William (Mac) McIlmoyl, Phil Toohey, George Ghindes, Mark Howe, Eric Berghorn, Kurt Jensen, Harrison Hood, Chris Cole, Tanya Fisher, Vicki Greenbaum, Kevin Powell, Ed Henicle, Floyd Hayes, Armin Fisher and Julie Lazar. I have had the rare and great good fortune to have never lost a climbing companion in the mountains in 50 years of endeavor.

Thanks to Bruce Hope who left a blank climbing journal in a duffel along with a pile of climbing gear on my doorstep. My journals are treasures and key references. Thanks to my father John who took us kids camping from our earliest ages, but never surmised I'd take the annual camping trip and turn it into a lifelong avocation. To my mother Barbara, a strong hiker and lover of the outdoors, who innocently gave me a copy of Hervey Voge's Climber's Guide to the High Sierra at sixteen, years before I imagined being a climber. Thanks to George Smith, George Russel and Jack Crowther my Explorer Scout leaders and all my fellow scouts Roger Eldridge, Dave Russel, Mercy Russel, Pat Moore, Greg Boone, Doug Corsette, Dave Smith, and Craig Smith. We had such great times while learning the skills and judgement needed for safe and successful mountain travel.

I was fortunate to find editor Michael Upchurch whose patience and professionalism are most appreciated. Thanks to my publisher Eric Johnson at Alive Book Publishing who has made the transition from manuscript to book form an easy process. Lastly thanks to my life partner Julie Lazar who helped me to focus, shape and edit my manuscript, and whose encouragement, love and faith have been instrumental in its completion.

Contents

Introduction ix
Chapter 1 Bridgework 19
Chapter 2 Exum 33
Chapter 3 Crossroads 43
Chapter 4 Quest for the Fourteeners 53
Chapter 5 Steve 75
Chapter 6 East Buttress of El Capitan 85
Chapter 7 The Sur 93
Chapter 8 Tenaya: Yosemite's Lost Canyon 101
Chapter 9 El Capitan: Viva Los Chicos Viajos 109
Chapter 10 The Dolomites 121
Chapter 11 Down Canyon 135
Chapter 12 Half Dome: Fifth Time is the Charm .. 149
Chapter 13 Jammin' Glacier 163
Chapter 14 Pigeon Spire Solo 183
Chapter 15 The Trinity and Mr. B 191
Chapter 16 Karakoram 201

Introduction

*Formative years - T-Crack,
Gibraltar Rock, Santa Barbara*

The first question which you will ask and which I must try to answer is this, "What is the use of climbing Mount Everest?" and my answer must at once be, "It is no use." There is not the slightest prospect of any gain whatsoever. Oh, we may learn a little about the behavior of the human body at high altitudes, where there is only a third of an atmosphere, and possibly medical men may turn our observation to some account for the purposes of aviation. But otherwise nothing will come of it. We shall not bring back a single bit of gold or silver, not a gem, nor any coal or iron. We shall not find a foot of earth that can be planted with crops to raise food. It's no use.

So, if you cannot understand that there is something in man which responds to the challenge of this mountain and goes out to meet it, that the struggle is the struggle of life itself upward and forever upward, then you won't see why we go. What we

> get from this adventure is just sheer joy. And joy is after all the end of life. We do not live to eat and make money. We eat and make money to be able to enjoy life. That is what life means and what life is for.
> —George Leigh Mallory, *Climbing Everest: The Complete Writings of George Mallory*

My first act of liberation that I can remember came at the age of two—a daring escape from my crib in the back bedroom of our modest suburban Los Angeles home, curious to see what lay beyond my view down the hallway. Two years later my parents took us to Woodside, California to visit relatives on their small ranch outside town. I am told my stubborn little four-year-old self didn't want to engage in some group activity, so I simply wandered off to explore the unfamiliar grounds. The adults got a bit frantic when I went missing. It was around this time that I also thought it would be fun to scare the living daylights out of my neighbor by positioning myself at the bottom of her trash can and pretending to be dead just before she brought it in from the curb.

Even then my spirit knew the conventional world would not be enough, that it would take some cage-rattling to carve out a bit of autonomy.

As a young boy and teen, I was good at knocking the ball around a tennis court or a baseball field. It looked like I was headed down the conventional-sports rabbit hole when at fifteen I had a tremendous stroke of luck—a friend on the tennis team invited me to join Explorer Post 356X, whose sole mission was to immerse kids in the world of mountains and mountaineering. On my first High Sierra adventure, we topped Bishop Pass at 12,000 feet and plunged into the glacially carved paradise of Dusy Basin. Two thousand feet above, the dark, serrated peaks of the Palisades towered over us, destined to become my favorite alpine climbing in California. Dusy Creek ripped and roared its way toward the Middle Fork Kings River, bounding over granite falls framed by penstemon and columbine. The spring runoff was high and wild that year and the very trail became a tributary stream for hundreds of yards. I had never experienced anything so alive before. It was like getting my hands on the Holy Grail.

And that was the moment, the epiphany. Right then, I knew I'd be returning to the mountains for the rest of my life.

In the Arthurian legend, the youthful Parsifal gets a peek into the Grail Castle, only to spend his whole life seeking a return. I was lucky to never leave that castle. Mountains have saved my life. Without them, I might have gone into ethically riskier occupations like pot growing or the military. I have found refuge, solace, adventure. and romance in every kind of natural environment, from the Bugaboos to the Dolomites, from the Sea of Cortez to Bristol Bay, on vertical rock walls, and in Southwest labyrinth canyons, and when I'm home, my garden is also a refuge. We forget sometimes that nature is the source of everything, and that civilization would fall to dust without it. By keeping a foot in both worlds, the natural and the human-made, I managed to retain a measure of balance in these crazy times.

I began climbing right at the end of the golden age of climbing in Yosemite (1950–70), just as environmental consciousness went global with the first Earth Day in 1970. Doug Robinson's article on the clean climbing ethic appeared in the Chouinard's Great Pacific Ironworks catalog in 1972, and the next year Galen Rowell and friends climbed Half Dome's Northwest Face without crack-scarring pitons, proving big walls could be climbed clean. The shift from the use of pitons to crack-friendly chocks was so abrupt that I never learned to drive a piton properly. The first camming devices (Friends) weren't available until 1977 so between 1971 and 1976 you were left with stoppers and hexes, both passive protection that took a great deal of skill to place properly and whose application range was limited. We compensated by getting bold—if the gear placements sucked, we just didn't bother to place any, sometimes leading out 50 feet or more above our last piece. I became quite good at that sort of thing in my youthful days when immortality seemed achievable.

In my twenties, I lived in Santa Barbara and spent as much time on the area's sandstone cliffs as I did trying to make a buck. Money was short and sometimes living in my truck was the only option. I never minded this at all. When a pair of climbing shoes wore out, cross-trainer sneakers substituted for half a year. A friend of mine who couldn't afford a rope learned to climb solo. If you couldn't afford a harness you used a swami belt—three-inch wide nylon webbing wound around your waist. And if you didn't have a rappel device you wrapped the rope around you in the Dulfersitz method or used a four-carabiner brake system. Sometimes we made our own gear, like the time we fashioned wired mashies and bashies for aid climbing with a friend's swage gun. We practiced minimalism and were proud of it. Our simple philosophy was summed up by phrases like, 'Suck it up', and 'No pain, no gain'. This was the atmosphere my friends and I grew up with. We were far from world-class climbers pushing the known boundaries, but at that time climbing was still a fringe sport and we loved being part of this exciting young movement.

Back then there weren't many opportunities to learn climbing. The Sierra Club's Rock Climbing Section, so influential in teaching climbers safe techniques in the '40s and '50s, was phased out in the '60s. Climbing schools were rare, climbing gyms were decades away, and Royal Robbins *Basic Rockcraft* was about the only book on the subject. Guidebooks to climbing areas were rare too, so you learned by word of mouth, roughly drawn sketches made by friends, or you eye-balled a new or unfamiliar route and just went for it. Bolt use was minimal and frowned on, and top-down inspection of routes was very bad manners. Within this milieu my friends and I were very clear about the subject of guiding—you might aspire to become a

Introduction

guide, but to hire one meant you were a duffer and it went against our independent philosophy. Besides, it was prohibitively expensive. My opinion was destined to change.

Almost every climber contemplating his first foray onto Yosemite's famed granite walls feels the fear like an eight-pound shot put in the bowels. From an initial, thorough intimidation of Yosemite walls, I made my first tentative explorations on short climbs and moved on to longer moderate routes, like Snake Dike, Overhang Bypass, Royal Arches, and my first Grade IV, Fairview Dome's regular route. Always foremost as a goal, but seemingly ever out of reach, were the big walls, which I hungered and lusted for, but feared greatly.

My desire to do the big walls began with the encouragement of a friend in the spring of 1977. He had just completed the Northwest Face of Half Dome. The climb entails a long and difficult approach, over 2,000 feet of climbing and a long descent. He told my partner and me that we could do it and I believed him. Almost. It would take five attempts over 25 years to realize that dream. Though a long time coming, the dream kept me motivated to stay in shape over that quarter of a century.

Spurred on by the 'fast and light' ethic gaining momentum at that time, a friend and I threw ourselves at the Chouinard/Herbert route on Yosemite's Sentinel Rock in late May 1985. We were hoping to do a one-day ascent of this difficult, 1,600-foot route, yet spent a near-freezing, shelter-less night on Chessman Pinnacle only a third of the way up and retreated the next morning. Four years later another friend and I had completed two-thirds of the Steck/Salathe (a classic testpiece also on the Sentinel) when darkness fell. Again, a freezing night of misery followed, huddled together back to back with one of those nearly useless emergency blankets thrown over our heads. We refrained from dipping into our meager supply of food and water, saving it for the following day's climbing. But in the morning, while edging around a tight spot, a faulty waist belt buckle sent our fanny pack carrying those supplies on a thousand-foot ride to the bottom. Another long, ignominious retreat followed. That —along with an earlier bivouac on the Grand Teton—was my third freezing bivouac in eleven years. I made a resolution: NO MORE EPICS! Maybe I just didn't have the brawn or the gumption to climb big walls.

In 1986 I met Armin Fisher through a series of serendipitous events destined to change everything (see Chapter XII). We began our climbing relationship as co-leaders but soon my new friend was leading most pitches. He was faster than anyone I knew by a factor of three. Suddenly, I was doing harder routes, longer routes, and doing them faster than ever. A new part of the climbing world was opening up.

In mid-October 1992, Armin and I climbed the South Face of Washington Column, a thousand-foot prow of granite hulking over the splendid meadows of upper Yosemite Valley. It was my first big wall, a dream come true, so perfect and satisfying that dreams of Half Dome faded for a while.

Shortly after, Armin moved to Italy to become a fully certified mountain guide, the only American to ever qualify. I spent my time alpine climbing in the Sierra Nevada, the Bugaboos of British Columbia, and the Wind Rivers of Wyoming. In 1997 a serious injury sidelined me for four months and with time to reflect, I realized time was running out for life dreams as I approached fifty. What could be more natural than to employ my friend and climbing mentor Armin to achieve these long-delayed and cherished dreams? Long-held opinions on hiring a guide vanished in face of necessity.

In a short six-year period that lasted until 2004, the biggest and in some ways the best climbs and experiences of my life came to pass. We climbed the Leaning Tower in 1998, The Nose on El Capitan, and the Constantini/Appolonia in the Dolomites of Italy in 2000. Then in 2002, 25 years after my first attempt, Half Dome by Northwest Face. A one-day ascent of the Steck Salathe in 2004 at age 54 was my big wall swansong.

What is it that draws people to climb mountains, an activity with inherently high risk and low material reward? Why do we return again and again to the vertical world? Every time we go, even to a short practice cliff, we risk injury or worse. Some of the greatest climbers in the world have met their end that way. John Bacher, perhaps the greatest free soloist of his generation, fell to his death on a familiar crag near his hometown of Mammoth, California. Lionel Terray, a master of the alpine environment, met his end on an easy climb near his home in France.

The apparent uselessness of the sport baffles many—ascend a giant pile of shifting rocks, get out of breath, freeze your ass off, see the dizzying world below, then worry all the way down as night approaches. All these things have happened to me and worse. What possible benefits could there be to offset all this unpleasantness?

When I was 49 we did the Nose route on Yosemite's El Capitan. It took us the best part of four days to accomplish. The higher we climbed the more we became attuned to our environment. We were not just visitors there, but temporary inhabitants of the vertical plane. The last third, the last 1,000 feet of El Cap rears up to slightly overhanging so that your view below includes the vast sweep of the concavity of the wall, forming a massive 3,000-foot 'C'. All our senses became heightened. We came upon startling surprises—flower gardens nurtured by seep water, lizards and frogs living their lives out on ledges and in cracks, the afternoon wind blowing a refreshing gale sweeping right through body and soul. One could hardly be more alive than on a big climb like this.

Then on our last day, on belay with three ropes at my feet, the east wind suddenly blew one rope off the ledge while I was paying out the lead rope to Armin. The free rope quickly disentangled itself from its coils and straightened out to its full 180 feet at a horizontal. I had never seen a rope do this in 30 years of climbing. The wind seemed to have planted a spark of life in that rope as it moved and twisted and gyrated through the air. Then, as I watched mesmerized, the end of the rope was further blown around a buttress of rock and disappeared from sight. Why this should have affected me so I don't know, but the surrealness of the scene was a transcendent moment, and I was grateful beyond measure to be a witness to such beauty in my life.

Lit by the afternoon light, the rock in the upper dihedrals that soared a thousand feet to the rim became like living, breathing things and I knew I was lucky to be present in one of the greatest cathedrals on earth. These are the reasons I think that we as climbers keep going. One has to push hard, endure pain and privation, overcome doubt, anxiety, fear, even terror, to get to a place of transcendent beauty. Beauty is in the eye of the beholder, but also in one's heart. You can't just rappel over the edge of El Cap and expect the same experience. The difference is in the journey, and how much we are willing to risk.

Telling stories is one of humankind's oldest pastimes. In writing and sharing these stories I hope to inspire others similarly inclined, to push on past fear and pursue their cherished goals. God knows how often I have been stricken nearly immobile by fear before a big climb, haggard from a sleepless night, and ready to bail with the flimsiest excuse. Sometimes that voice is wise, warning me away from true danger, but nearly always it is fear and nothing else. And that by pushing on, the greatest climbs and times of my life were just ahead.

For 35 years the mountains had inspired and catapulted me into and beyond my dreams. But where do you go when the show ends, the candle flame dims and you are confronted with the realities of an aging body? The hollow place I felt as my climbing career wound down would not last long. I had done a few, very select river trips like the Middle Fork of the Salmon in Idaho in 1975 and two weeks on the Colorado through the Grand Canyon in 1987. Despite my climbing bias, I considered this latter outing the finest of a lifetime up to that point. Everyone should have the opportunity to run the Colorado at least once in their lives. These were commercial trips in which everything was taken care of for a price. It was not affordable to do often.

But then a float trip in Labyrinth Canyon on the Green River of Utah with my old climbing partner Robin in 2005 really opened my eyes. Instead of fighting gravity, we were going with the flow of the river, and instead of dragging a haul bag up vertical walls, we could allow the boat to be our mule. There were just three of us on that trip, we were completely self-contained, and the cost was minimal. This kind of private boat adventure was accessible nearly anytime, and suddenly a new passion was born. It made me realize how much I needed the water element in my life. I've been whitewater boating for 15 years now and the thrill and satisfaction I feel on the river is just as wonderful as what I used to feel on the crags.

Somewhere in our dim prehistory, an incipient crack appeared in the relationship between Homo sapiens and the rest of life on earth. Some say it began with the dawn of civilization, some further back when we began hunting animals. In any case, the crack has widened over some thousands of years and is now an abyss that threatens our species and others. Fifty-five percent of the world's population lives in urban areas, a number that is set to rise much higher in the coming decades. Many are bereft of the opportunity to experience the mystery and awe of wild places and the healing energy that comes with time spent in our ancestral home, nature. The cure seems obvious, but the path to forging a new relationship with Earth is fraught with pitfalls.

Mountaineering and wilderness river travel are two ways to reconnect. Not only do they challenge mind, body, and our emotional nature but they are touchstones for the spirit, a pathway back home. My advice to climbers and river runners is to have your goals, make your tick lists, but don't forget why you're out there. Your personal connection to the Earth, (your grounding), the beauty and mystery found in the outdoors should be primary. As we age, the need for thrills diminishes, our connection to the universe, the earth, the plants, and animals becomes deeper, stronger, quieter, more resonant.

Whatever lies in store for the future, I know I'll never lose my connection to the natural, elemental world that is for me, the only real, tangible source of life itself.

Chapter 1
Bridgework

A good scare is worth more to a man than good advice.
    —Ed Howe

This little adventure took place in 1972, a far more innocent age than today. A similar attempt today might end in arrest on suspicion of terrorism, not loitering as we were charged. During research for this story, my request for basic information on Cold Springs Arch Bridge was denied by the Office of Homeland Security.

It was a cool, bright February afternoon and from the prow of massive sandstone that jutted out into the one-lane road creating a bottleneck, you could see the blue Pacific as it lay sparkling and twinkling in the sun, two thousand feet below. Up the road a mile was Painted Cave State Historic Park, an ancient site sacred to the Chumash Indians. A stout, iron-barred gate blocks the entrance to the permanently shadowed cave, which holds pictographs I never could make out due to the darkness. The gate prevents vandals from spray-painting graffiti over the sacred but mysterious drawings, symbols that were drawn over four hundred years ago whose meaning has been lost to time.

Our little rock pile hadn't been spared the touch of modern graffitists, but it had the advantage of various low- and highball climbing routes. Twenty feet above the rocky and uneven ground (long before the days of crash pads), Bruce high-stepped to place a toe on a wrinkle of rock. Fingertips pressing on dime edges, he drew himself up to full height. I was spotting below, hoping to break his fall if a foot slipped or if the notoriously fragile sandstone failed. Now reaching with both hands to a shallow dish, Bruce first inverted one hand then the other, so his palms were in full contact with the rock. With spread fingers acting as stabilizers, he trusted all his weight, brought one leg up, then the other, to match his hands and slowly, evenly, again stood to full height. With his long reach, he was able to grasp the rim and pull to safety.

"You wanna give it another go?"

"Nah, I'm pumped." My forearms were tight and bulging from hours of work like this.

"We still have two hours of daylight. Let's check out that arch bridge at Cold Springs."

Bruce and I had met in the early fall at the first meeting of the University of California Santa Barbara mountaineering club. As the more experienced climber, he fell easily into the role of my climbing mentor, and we often dashed off for weekends in Joshua Tree, Pinnacles, and the Sespe country above Ojai. Six foot three, astute, and smart as a rawhide whip, Bruce at twenty-one had the jaded worldviews of a much older person. His favorite expression for the foibles of mankind, say, whenever a driver merged dangerously on the freeway or a climber risked his life through poor judgment, was "Incompetence is *rank*!"

Once in a crowded Yosemite campground, we grabbed the last site, ate our meal, and put everything away, leaving his Volkswagen as our claim to the site. Returning from the campfire talk well after dark, we found not one, but *two* massive recreational vehicles usurping our camp, both tables littered with camping gear, children running amok, the adults slinging beers, and the whole phantasmagoria lit by a string of high-powered halogen lights. I was furious but to my added consternation, Bruce was highly amused. We crawled into our sleeping bags on the far side of the car to block the lights, my friend laughing

Chapter 1

crazily, delighted this latest experience matched his view of the world.

I sat in the passenger seat of the canary-yellow Superbeetle and inspected my hands—in sharp contrast to sun-browned arms they were a rough, florid red from wrist to fingers. Someone, maybe it was Bruce, once described young climbers as daredevils with the hands of seventy-year-old men. With a loop of nylon webbing, I practiced tying the ring bend knot, looping it through itself like an infinity sign, while we took Painted Cave Road back down to the highway. In the lean, winter afternoon light, Santa Barbara lay nestled between the mountains and ocean, glowing with a golden light. Its various neighborhoods—the Riviera, the Mesa, Samarkand, the beachfront with Stearn's Wharf—were all visible from our vantage point.

Ten miles to the west, situated on a bluff between the Goleta Slough and the ocean, was my home, the University of California, Santa Barbara (UCSB), with its lagoon, acres of open space, and trademark Storke tower. The only smudge on the panorama was suburban Goleta, mistaken sprawl that stole some of the best avocado and citrus land in the state. Geographically isolated, Santa Barbara is close to Point Concepcion, that wind and wave-battered promontory that deflects the cold Humboldt Current out to sea, allowing surfers in Southern California the luxury of dispensing with wetsuits. My adopted town had everything—beauty, recreation, social and intellectual life, and something else you felt downtown on a summer evening, a palpable, feminine, seductive ambiance. I didn't think I'd ever leave.

Cold Spring Arch Bridge

Our deserted, switch-backing road led to Highway 154, an alternate to 101 cutting through rural Santa Ynez Valley, famed as a center for raising thoroughbred horses. At the top of San Marcos Pass, a few scattered houses and cabins sheltered under brows of shadowed sandstone. We pulled off at Stagecoach Road, came to a turnout, tumbled out for a view, and stood transfixed. Like a leap of the imagination, twin steel arches drew a rainbow-curved arch a thousand feet from one side of Cold Spring Canyon to the other. Dwarfed by the distance, the live oak trees in the creek bottom looked like ground cover. The bridge's understructure, painted a spring green, blended with the natural colors around it. Connecting the arches with the flat line of the highway was, from our viewpoint, a strut-work delicate as a lattice. Despite the steel and concrete, the bridge seemed less to muscle its way across but rather to float ethereally

Chapter 1

above the canyon. Seen perhaps in the misty light of dawn, one might be reminded of Tolkien's Middle Earth, where trolls and elves pass over a gossamer framework suspended between jutting rock towers.

Unfortunately, due less to the guard railings than perspective, the average motorist is clueless as they pass over the longest steel span arch in the state. Below them is a drop of four hundred feet to the tree-shrouded canyon bottom, nearly twice the spell-binding distance sightseers get from the Golden Gate Bridge. We stood for ten minutes admiring the architect's vision.

"Let's get a beer at the Inn," suggested my ever-practical friend.

Nestled into a crook in the old highway was the Stagecoach Inn directly opposite the bridge downstream. This was the original 1880s log cabin, dark and squat, brooding under a jungle canopy of live oaks. It all but disappeared into its surroundings. Inside it was dim like a bear's lair, hazy with stale old cigarettes and wood smoke from the blackened stone fireplace. No one was around. Our eyes adjusting to the light, we looked at old black and white photos on the wall, the rough-hewn wood furniture, the long, oak-paneled bar. Still, no one came. We left thirsty and walked down the road toward the bridge.

As we approached, we saw two of the four massive concrete thrust blocks supporting the twin arches on a steep and brushy hillside. The spans, nearly level at the center of the bridge, pitched slowly downward until plunging into the thrust blocks at a fifty-degree angle. Every thirty feet, round, one-foot diameter struts connected the arches to the understructure of the two-lane blacktop that lay on top almost like an afterthought.

"You know, Kenny boy, it looks like someone could walk those arches if they wanted to."

"Walk?" I said incredulously, "what about that angle at either end?"

"That", said Bruce, "will take some climbing. Let's take a look."

A steep, loose climb through brush led to the thrust block. The angle didn't look so bad from here. We measured the width of the span with outstretched arms. I could just barely wrap fingertips around both ends, but Bruce with his reach could get a full finger wrap. It was a stretch for sure, but by using counterforce in a bear hug and friction-ing with the feet…

"Make a couple of moves, Bruce, see if it's slick."

He did. It was smooth but not slick.

Back on the road, we stood in awe and admiration, torn by fear and desire. Did we dare catwalk the arch, dance above the abyss? Were we hearing the siren call of this beauty, or were we confusing it with the sound of a distant highway patrol car? We let the question hang in the twilight as we sped down the pass and the scattered lights of Goleta came on one by one like earthbound stars.

A couple of months passed. By coincidence, we were both geography majors and shared a class called Spatial Analysis, a study of abstract theorems and concepts that underlay our chosen discipline. Because Bruce grasped these abstruse ideas so quickly and I never did, we had plenty of time to review our last adventure and plan the next one. The vision of that simple but elegant arch bridge over Cold Spring Canyon wouldn't go away. We agreed to meet one Saturday morning before sunrise while most of the student body would be sleeping off the effects of the obligatory Friday night party.

Climbing man-made structures wasn't new to us. Buildering was convenient when the rocks were too far away. Bruce and his friend Wayne had scaled the east face of the five-story Engineering Building at UCSB at night using skyhooks and cliffhangers. I started examining campus buildings and found the architects had left all kinds of route possibilities: a delicate traverse on shallow indentations at the University Center; an off-width chimney between two, concrete pillars underneath Storke Tower (students referred to it as Storke's erection); and face climbing that led to a

Chapter 1

wild but easy overhang on the mid-campus cafeteria.

From old texts in the library I learned we were part of a collegiate tradition dating back to the early 1900s, where students at England's Cambridge and Oxford universities made daring night forays, leaving effigies of the dean on the tiptop of the multi-story cathedral to the consternation of the administration. (If caught, their punishment would have meant expulsion. At our school, no one paid any attention.) Here was a precedent for our behavior and our plan to climb the arch bridge was simply taking the next logical step.

We sped over the nearly empty highway before the sun rose, following closely the route that John C. Fremont had used over a hundred years ago to surprise a regiment of the Mexican army at Gaviota Pass. No cover of fog favored us this morning but at least all was quiet. We parked the bug on Old Stagecoach Road, grabbed our gear, and scrambled up the crumbly hillside to the north abutment. I was anxious to turn the nervous goblin churning in my gut into action. With the rope in a neat, coiled pile at my feet, my anchor a sling tied to a girder, I looped a bight of rope around my waist, clipped either side into my harness with carabiners for a body belay, and was ready.

"Go Bruce," I said, "You're on."

My partner stretched one arm out, then the other, fingers curling around the span's edges, applying counter pressure in a bear hug, placed a shoe on cool steel, and took the first step. When both feet matched, he moved both hands higher, and the feet followed suit, knees nearly to his chest due to the high angle of the span. He made identical moves for thirty feet until reaching the first strut. Half-hitching a long, perlon sling, he attached a carabiner through the end and clipped his rope.

"Nice goin'," I said, easing my grip on the rope.

After 150 feet the rope came tight, the anchor was set and it was my turn. I felt the welded edges of the span, knurled like steel caterpillars on the inside of my fingers, rough enough for purchase but without danger of metal splinters. The ground dropped away three times as fast as I rose and soon the old highway was a hundred feet below. Compared to rock climbing, it was unnerving to have exposure on *both* sides but also exhilarating. Just don't slip off this thing you fool, I thought, or you'll have an embarrassing dangle in space. (In fact, a fall would have meant a wild pendulum underneath the bridge with nothing to climb but the rope. We both carried two prussic loops in case.) Each welcoming upright strut I approached was like a big, dry rock in a swift river crossing, and wrapping an arm around it, enjoyed the relative security before moving on.

Occasionally a car would pass underneath us on Old Stagecoach Road. I exchanged belay stances with Bruce (I wasn't leading yet), passed over the slings he'd reuse, and off he went, more quickly now due to the lessening angle of the span. Fifty feet of rope was paid out when a loud noise attracted our attention. It was a projected voice on a bullhorn.

"Get down from the bridge. This is the police!"

Our attention was so focused we hadn't noticed the arrival of a squad car on the bluff above the north end of the main highway. Two uniformed officers were standing next to it. The command was repeated.

"Take in the rope, Ken, I'm coming back."

The game was up. By the time we reversed our moves and scrambled back to the old highway, Santa Barbara's finest were waiting.

"We had a report from a passing motorist there were suicide jumpers on the bridge."

Bruce assured them we were competent, trained climbers, and knew exactly what we were doing. He fell into the role of liaison like an old diplomat and soon we were chatting and joking good-naturedly about the incident.

"Well, boys, we have to hand you something so we're giving you a notice to appear in court for loitering. Court date will be

Chapter 1

in about two weeks. Probably won't be a big deal." The cop gave us a wink.

With an amazing presence of mind, Bruce pulled out a Kodak brownie camera.

"Mind if I immortalize this on celluloid?"

They straightened their ties and one pulled a comb out of his pocket to spruce up. The old black and white photo shows one officer reclining in the front seat of the squad car with the door open, one leg casually resting on the ground, the other officer standing next to him mugging for the camera, and me, long hair and beard and wool cap, a rope over my shoulder, pleased as hell we're not headed for the county jail. Just out of sight soars the still virgin arch bridge, scene of the crime.

Santa Barbara's Finest and Me
Photo by Bruce Hope

The day of our court appearance was a bright sunny morning, but all I noticed was my interior landscape. I was a wreck having never been in court before or even in trouble with the law.

In contrast, Bruce was all confidence and business. The Santa Barbara County Courthouse is a magnificent affair, built in the Spanish style mandated for the city after the 1925 earthquake. It presents the appearance of a grand, Arabic fortress, with towers, arches, balconies, and enormous terra cotta tiles on the roof. Tall, spiky, Monkey Puzzle trees on the lawn outside lend scale to the three-story edifice. We walked through the massive sandstone archways softened by vivid magenta bougainvillea, into the semi-formal inner courtyard, lush foliage like banana trees and Australian tree ferns gave the impression of a King's Palace. If we had climbed the broad-stepped, sandstone stairway to the top, an observation deck would have presented a 360-degree view of the city—an Impressionist's interpretation of Spanish tiles in a forest of urban green.

In contrast to all this beauty, two armed guards led a gang of manacled, uniformed prisoners down the hallway. We stepped into the courtroom of Judge Lodge and sat.

"Let me do all the talking," said Bruce, "what's his name is a softie, we should be out of this soon."

He stood and spoke clearly in our defense, short, dark hair combed, neatly dressed, as everyone listened. The look on the Judge's face softened, then turned to a smile, and I detected some suppressed amusement from others in the courtroom. Compared to the handcuffed prisoners sitting alongside the wall, we were just two guys out on a lark.

Judge Lodge smiled benignly.

"I think you two have been through enough. I'm going to drop these charges but, a final warning," and here the handsome Judge lowered his head a bit and the smile disappeared, "I don't want to see you in here again on the same charge."

"Yes sir!" we chorused.

We flushed from the court like quail.

Two years later we both graduated from UCSB. Bruce moved on to USC for a master's degree and me to a bohemian life of

Chapter 1

partial employment living in the student ghetto of Isla Vista. Climbing was now the focus of my life. My new partner Warren and I were temperamentally attuned to the lifestyle, dashing off at every opportunity, ever in search of new rock. He was tall, well over six feet, long blond hair to his waist, hyper-kinetic on the rock. At the end of a hard day, he liked to down a six-pack of Heineken dark and the largest bar of Cadbury milk chocolate he could find. In the garage on Olive Street was his pet project, a life-size Ben Franklin robot he put together from scratch in his spare time. Eventually, he had it moving and talking and spouting aphorisms like "the early bird gets the first ascent."

Together, Warren and I bushwhacked carnivorous chaparral to obscure sandstone domes in the local hills, made midnight runs to Tahquitz Rock in his Coronet 440 station wagon, and scared ourselves silly tandem free-soloing three hundred-foot routes at Sespe Gorge. One day I mentioned a bridge route that needed finishing and the project was back on the front burner. This time, we had to make sure no one stopped us.

Early on a Sunday morning, we parked the station wagon at the Stagecoach Inn, our packs concealing well the climbing hardware inside, and walked down the road, pretending to look for a hiking trail. We were dressed in green, the same color as the bridge. Under the bridge, we halted. Scanning the canyon, we checked for signs of life but even the highway above was quiet. Quickly, we scampered up the brushy hillside and ducked behind the same thrust block that Bruce and I had used for cover previously. On went the swami belts, one or sometimes two-inch wide nylon webbing that served as harnesses in those days. They were also green. We were going to merge with this thing like soldiers in the jungle. A ring bend knot was secured with a simple overhand on each side and off I went, leading this time, quickly.

With half the rope out, the road was already dizzyingly below when the sound of a car reached my ears. I immediately lay flat and unmoving, invisible, and the driver passed safely away and unaware down-canyon. Warren had been feeding the rope out conservatively, so no loops formed as it slid flat along the span. Only when the car was completely out of sight did I move again. We didn't want any would-be rescuers. When the full one hundred fifty feet was out, it was Warren's turn. Two more cars appeared simultaneously, running up- and down-canyon, and Warren spread-eagled the plank while I used the strut as partial cover. Once again, we went undetected, or so we hoped. Swapping leads was simple. When Warren reached me, he'd got all the gear except the anchor, so we played leapfrog.

The span's angle lessened with each foot gained and after four rope lengths, we were walking upright on the arch's level top. You'd have to have been a suicide jumper to blow it there. Suddenly I stopped cold and stood in wonder. The evidence at my feet was unmistakable—big, dusty footprints going in our direction. Had someone else had the same idea? Or were these the old boot prints of workmen? The bridge had been built a decade before and surely wind and rain would have washed the span clean by the time of our climb. I never did find the answer.

We stopped at the very center of the span and together marveled at the space around us, a 360-degree panorama, the exposure below intoxicating. We sat quietly and enjoyed it, knowing it was unlikely we would be here again. Vehicles passed directly above us, their occupants ignorant of the vast space below them and of the two humans perched like fledgling peregrines, doing their best version of flight. Our only distant view was the rugged San Rafael Mountains to the north, the condor's ancient habitat. Directly beneath our gaze was Cold Spring Creek, an opaque, silver ribbon meandering through its oaken matrix, sparkling here and there, too far away to hear its voice even with the highway quiet. We savored the moment, the nuttiness of the situation, sharing a chocolate bar. Soon enough it would be time to go.

The second half of the traverse was identical to the first, except that near the end where the span dips at 50°, we climbed backward, letting gravity do the work. Then it was over. No cops awaited us this time, only a steep scramble to the road. We repacked our gear and walked back to the Stagecoach Inn as if finishing a morning hike. No one seemed the wiser. Our car was still the only one at the Inn, which wouldn't be open for hours yet. It was 8 AM on a Sunday and we were famished. We headed into town to the Copper Coffee Pot to celebrate with an old-fashioned, high-fat breakfast.

"Warren, how many rope lengths was that, seven?"

"Yeah, seven."

"That's, let's see, a thousand and fifty feet altogether. Christ, if that was vertical rock it would've taken all day." End to end it had taken ninety minutes.

As the Coronet 440 topped San Marcos and the red-tiled roofs of Santa Barbara reappeared, I thought about the first attempt with Bruce, the court appearance, and remembering what the Judge had said—

"Don't show up again on the same charge."

I guess we kept our promise.

A version of this story first appeared in *Mountain Gazette* in 2002.

Chapter 2
Exum

Only those who will risk going too far can possibly find out how far they can go.
  —T.S. Eliot, from the preface to *Transit of Venus, Poems* by Harry Crosby

The most dangerous thing in mountaineering is certainly the carefree confidence of youth.
  —Lionel Terray

Our near ascent of the Grand Teton in winter-like conditions occasioned the first of four unplanned bivouacs in my life. All have been utterly miserable affairs in near or sub-freezing conditions. This first one was by far the worst. With no experience or knowledge of my abilities, I assumed I was entering a fatal situation. Thankfully, human beings are capable of far more than we understand. I returned to climb the Exum route in August 2002 and finally set foot on the summit. In marked contrast to that first foray, it was a pleasant and casual day on the crags.

It was early June 1978, and Warren, Jeanna, and I were crammed into the bench seat of my Ford Courier on our way to the Tetons as our first stop in a summer-long road trip. Our first objective was the classic Exum route on the Grand Teton. My only other mountaineering outing of note had been just the week before on the north side of Mt. Shasta. On the five-day effort, we had experienced whiteouts, gale-force winds, and deep snows from approach to summit. In a summit photo, my face is grossly contorted by 70 mph winds as the rope blows out at a horizontal angle. Warren had even less experience than me. Up until now, we had been strictly 'fun in the sun' rock climbers. What Warren and I lacked in snow and ice work would have to be compensated for in youthful energy.

The American Alpine Club's climbers ranch in Moose, Wyoming offered log cabins for only $5 a night, even though we are not yet members. It was so early in the season that few climbers were there, meaning the three of us had a cabin to ourselves for most of a week. It felt like paradise.

The climbing ranger at the Visitor Center had some news that should have sobered us but didn't—no one had completed an ascent of the Grand that year due to winter-like conditions and deep snows. No matter. With youthful optimism, we just knew the weather was going to clear up especially for us. From our meager supply of funds, we bought the *Climber's Guide to the Teton Range* and thumbed to the Exum Ridge description. The author Leigh Ortenburger called it a Grade II, F4. We had been climbing up to 5.10 (F 10) in recent months on our sunny Santa Barbara crags. On paper, the Grand sounded pretty easy to us. We made the classic mistake of not figuring in the mountaineering variable. We would pay for it dearly.

The three of us started up Garnett Canyon, beginning at Lupine Meadows trailhead late the next day with full packs in overcast, cold and drippy weather. Nothing could dampen our spirits. As if in confirmation of our accord with nature, the sky cleared toward sunset. In the morning, Jeanna returned to the Climber's Ranch expecting to see us on the following evening. Fog blanketing the valley below cleared by late morning and a brilliant mountain day unfolded as we moved up-canyon through the heavy snowpack. The giant snowfield below the Lower Saddle was smothered in snow except for a patch of rocky medial moraine where we pitched our tent. Manny and Roger, who were camped just below, had experience on Denali

CHAPTER 2

and said the Exum should be easy by comparison.

Warren and I were buoyed by this news and retired early from the numbing cold, to prepare for a typically early alpine start of 4 AM. But around midnight we both awoke to a sound like the rustling of felt drumsticks on timpani. In surprise, I peeked outside and saw snow falling thickly all around us. We didn't know Rocky Mountain weather patterns, but in the Sierra, the mountains we knew best, it would mean a major weather event. Disappointed, we prepared for a long, tent-bound day.

Middle Teton from the Grand

At daybreak, I startled awake to the light, unzipped the North Face A-frame, and looked out to a brilliant, clear blue sky. Alpenglow torched a double peak to the west and I got the shot with my old Olympus rangefinder. But we'd missed our alpine start and I wondered aloud to Warren if we should wait a day.

"Nah, let's do it!"

We rushed madly through breakfast to get going. A few minutes' walk beyond our tent, the climb to the Lower Saddle began. We had to do without the assistance of the fixed cable which was completely snowed under. On top of the Lower Saddle was an empty, low profile Quonset hut used by Exum Guide Service guides and clients. Their season usually started in early July but this year it might begin even later. We briefly followed the standard Owen/Spalding route but soon veered right and climbed a ridge. Behind us, the Middle Teton glowed dazzling white in the early morning sun. Ahead was the obvious and impressive ramp called Wall Street, again completely snowed under. We picked our way carefully along the traverse as the exposure increased. The ramp ended and a snow-free gap of several feet separated us from the start of the Upper Exum Ridge. Below me was an exhilarating thousand feet of the Lower Exum Route. With ice axe looped over my arm, I placed my heavy mountaineering boots on small toe holds, then took a big step and pulled to safety.

From here on it would be almost impossible to match the guidebook's descriptions with the terrain. Nearly every pitch was snowed under or worse, iced up. Progress was slow and because we had neglected to bring crampons, dangerous on icy holds. The exception was a rare bit of bare rock called the Friction Pitch, considered the technical crux of the climb, but for us, it was a welcome respite and the easiest pitch of the day. We kept moving relentlessly without a thought for rest or food.

Chapter 2

Wall Street, Exum route, Grand Teton

Much later in the day, I stood alone on a snowy ridge, our clear morning skies quickly filling in with swiftly moving cumulus clouds. Above me, Warren had been out of sight and sound for an hour. The only sounds were the rising wind and my uneven breath. Everywhere I looked was wild looking snowscape, unlike any I'd ever seen. A much lower elevation Table Mountain was blanketed with the white stuff.

Chained to the anchor I felt intensely vulnerable and realized with a pang how time had slipped away. There had been no thought of, or preparations for, an overnight stay. A grade II F4? That should be a half day's effort. The danger of our overconfidence was hitting full force. We *must* get off this mountain, I thought. At last came the welcome words of *off belay* and warnings that the snow had turned to mush in the afternoon sun and the only belay he could find was inadequate. I catapulted myself up the snowfield, too full of adrenaline to heed his caution.

Another rope pitch above I found another suspect anchor in some loose rocks. When Warren joined me he was not alone. Roger and Manny were right behind him, the only other roped team on the Exum today. We hadn't seen them since Wall Street, and they seemed unusually quiet and confused and wanted to team up with us for safety. It became apparent that their Alaskan experience was minimal. I continued leading in a howling wind while huge cumulus massed and marched across the obscuring sky. The summit was not far now and the descent, we hoped, would be apparent from there. But the route presented a bewildering array of snow and rock hummocks. With the wind so strong down there, the summit would be enveloped in a maelstrom. Memories of the hurricane-force winds on Mt. Shasta were still fresh. Progress seemed futile and I returned dejected.

Our situation looked bleak. A retreat down the Exum was impossible and our present position untenable. Then Warren spied a wide ledge below us within a rope's distance. Perhaps there was still hope. I volunteered at once and disappeared over the edge. Immediately the raging wind cut me off from communication with the others. The ropes were barely long enough, but with some stretch, they landed me on a long, twenty-foot wide, down-sloping ledge. I didn't know it then, but by sheer dumb luck, I'd landed on the main rappel ledge for the descent from the Grand. I vainly shouted *off rappel* into the tempest and gave three strong rope tugs as a signal, donned gloves to warm my freezing hands, and hunkered down to wait. It was going to be a long one.

The sun was sinking into the western horizon through pillows of orange clouds by the time the others joined me an hour later. The delay was inexplicable and maddening. In the twilight pallor, all their faces had a look of resignation. There was no explanation for the delay, but I still wanted off this mountain. No one made a move to pull the ropes down. I grabbed one of the doubled lines and pulled with all my might with no success. The other line was just as stubborn, both held fast by the rapidly freezing snow.

All day I had been moving hard, driving myself with a whip, confident that with enough forward movement, we'd be off the mountain that night. The frustration of the previous hour and its useless waste was the last straw. I lost my composure and bounced on one rope with all the weight and will I could muster, screaming into the wind like a madman. It might have been funny in different circumstances. But losing one's composure in difficult alpine situations is the last thing you want. In my distress, I didn't see that the others had found a small alcove and were calmly preparing for the night.

It was then that I heard the voice. The message was as certain as sunrise: *Calm down, join your companions, be patient, and in the morning you will, without a shadow of a doubt, get up and walk off the mountain.* Or something close to that. Whether they were actual words or a thought-form, whether it came from inside my head or out, I'll never know. But rarely in life does one know something for absolute certainty. Call it a spirit guardian if you like. Though the promise wouldn't exempt me from an iota of suffering, there was no doubt in my mind of the outcome. It took only a nanosecond to go from hysteria to Zen, from paralyzing fear to utter peace. I let go of the rope and walked over to my companions, who hadn't noticed my temporary derangement.

The darkness swallowed the last gleams of light as we prepared for the long night. The alcove narrowed toward the back and opened in front—a shelter just large enough for three people. I had only a pair of nylon chaps over blue jeans and a Dacron jacket for warmth. We took anything extra like ropes and hardware and placed it under us for insulation. A tarp was produced for wind protection, but it was long enough to cover only three of us. The man in front was getting hammered by the wind so we settled on a game of musical chairs, switching positions every quarter-hour. Suddenly ravenous, I found some nuts and dried fruit in my jacket pocket intended for lunch and chowed down.

We didn't talk much that night, all of us thinking our own thoughts, fighting our own battles, yet still grateful for the others' presence. My feet were so cold I had to move my toes like a metronome all night, glad for something to focus on. I counted up to a hundred then started all over again. Around midnight, Roger got up and wandered off without saying much. I briefly wondered about his mental stability but said nothing. Eventually, he set up a hammock shelter of his own, attached to the rock wall, where he stayed for the remainder of the night.

The rest of us found favored positions: Warren at the front of the alcove where there was more room for his large frame; Manny stayed in the middle, garnering warmth from bodies on either side; and I, being the shortest, scrunched up in back farthest from the wind. Sometime in the night, I awoke with a start, toes like frozen blocks. It was a long time before any feeling came back to them. Slowly the wind seemed to be losing its force.

I must have slept an hour or two because suddenly it was dawn. Trying to rise, I felt like an arthritic old man. From outside, my little cubbyhole looked like a rheumatic's nightmare. The wind was still, no clouds sullied the skies and it looked to be a fine day. We'd all survived our first bivouac, and with that my energy returned with a rush. Warren was suffering from partial snow blindness after losing track of his sunglasses the day before, later to be found in a jacket pocket. I took a half-hour to Prusik back to the anchor where I confirmed the ropes were frozen solid, broke them free from the snow, and hurried back down. But it was no use. The frigid air immediately sealed them once again over a large lip of snow.

When it came down to it, leaving expensive ropes was quite easy. Resigned to the loss, the anchor was soon found at the end of the ledge and we all rappelled using the two remaining 120-

foot ropes. The final 60 feet was a free abseil, floating a long way from the undercut cliff. The ropes were short by 15 feet and the first three rappelers had slid off both lines to fall free to a snowy platform. As the last man, I made sure to hang onto one end as the ropes slid through my rappel device. With the tension going through the anchor above, I floated to the ground like a parachutist, rope in hand. If I had failed to do so, we'd have lost a second set of ropes.

The Owen Spalding descent route was straightforward, a couloir of frozen sun cups. By midday our camp on the glacial moraine came into view, islanded by a sea of snow. A long, fast, and delightful glissade took us to our tattered tent. The high winds of yesterday had broken one of the poles and the rain fly seams were ripped. Roger and Manny spent an hour picking up pieces of their tent strewn about the snowfield for several hundred yards.

To my surprise, Warren continued down to the trailhead, worried about Jeanna who was expecting us to show the night before. Manny and Roger retired and I didn't see them until we met in the Cowboy Bar in Jackson Hole two days later. One of the more serene and blissful afternoons of my life followed. The day was warm and inviting. I cooked a small meal, watched as huge blocks of ice came shattering down the cliff in an icefall, and took a slow meditative walk to a water source to fill my canteen. A woman appeared with a white mask of zinc oxide on her face for sun protection, smeared from ear to ear, giving her a comical look that did not hide her good looks. Her friends were coming down from the Exum and excitedly she tried to kiss her boyfriend, who pushed her away.

"Get away from me with that stuff!"

It didn't dampen her spirits at all. No, they hadn't seen our ropes, and yes, they too found the guidebook useless due to the heavy snow conditions. They made the first ascent of the Grand that year sound easy. The year before they had climbed

Mt. Robson in Canada and seemed a bit condescending after hearing about our struggles. It didn't dampen my spirits either. After the tumult of the previous days, simple existence was plenty.

That night I donned every piece of clothing I had and crawled into my sleeping bag, open to the sky. In the morning I was in no hurry to leave my camp of such good feelings. Heading down late morning I soon came upon a lovely sight—the zinc oxide lady, ice axe in hand, perfecting her glissade technique wearing only a short-sleeve top and some skimpy underpants.

We spent a few more days of R and R at the Climber's Ranch, offering a modest reward to other climbers to retrieve our ropes. Here in the valley, the sun was warm and the skies blue. But up there on the heights winter had returned to the Tetons and no one was able to get close. It may have been weeks before another ascent of the Grand was possible.

Chapter 3
Crossroads

Good judgment comes from experience. Experience comes from bad judgment.
—Evan Hardin

I assure you it's harder to battle human stupidity than to do battle with mountains. Mountains, after all, have holds.
—Erhard Loretan, *Night Naked: A Climber's Autobiography*

One winter day in 1981, I found myself talking to the preeminent mountaineer Paul Petzoldt by telephone. He nearly had me convinced to take his five-week mountaineering guide course in the Tetons that coming summer. The $800 fee was a quarter of my annual income but my life needed a decision. I was a half-time climbing bum as I started my third decade of life, scratching a living from a landscape business, and at this point homeless while camping in a friend's living room a month before my annual summer road trip. I'd been living this life for seven years, ever since graduating from university, but the specter of my thirtieth year was a dark shadow over my conscience. Shouldn't I have been finding some career?

Paul, now a legendary figure in American mountaineering, was a climbing bum himself in his younger years. As a raw 16-year-old novice he made an early ascent of the Grand Teton, his footwear a pair of trusty cowboy boots for kicking steps in the snow and ice. He then founded the first climbing guide service in the Tetons. On his first trip to the Himalaya in 1938, he almost made the first ascent of K2, the second-highest peak in the world. Later he founded the National Outdoor Leadership School. Being a rascal, he had gotten himself kicked out and by 1977 had a new school called Wilderness Education Association (WEA).

"Ken, I guarantee you'll have a great time, hang the money, you need to do this."

The Petzoldt lodge in Driggs, Idaho was a rambling three-story affair whose oversize fireplace has its heat piped to all levels, making it cozy even in the harsh winters. Guide hopefuls, men and women in equal numbers, came from all over the country. The lodge could sleep an army battalion, but I opted to spend the night on the top deck, open to the sky. In a full 360-degree circle, bursts of silent heat lightning, like distant artillery fire, exposed the wild, jagged forms of dark peaks.

"If you don't like the weather, wait five minutes," Paul liked to say.

June in Idaho can be like winter in California. As I stood outside the wilderness outfitter's storefront in tiny downtown Driggs, brilliant sun alternated with freezing wind and a furious hailstorm. We were warned to bring only wool clothing for the five-week outing. WEA provided tents, sleeping bags, and cookware, all of the sturdiest variety. A tent weighed twelve pounds and the down bag would keep you warm in an Alaskan winter. My backpack clocked in at seventy pounds, twice as heavy as anything I had carried in fifteen summers, yet many others were heavier, 80 even 90 pounds, and the women were not spared.

The first ten days we occupied the same camp on the little-known west side of the Tetons. It was a shakedown period to learn the basics of wilderness survival, give the group time to bond, and, for the students and instructors, to get to know one another. One cool, overcast day, Paul, a huge bear of a man, well over six feet and some 200 pounds, stood before us wearing a red Pendleton and demonstrating how to light a fire when everything is soaked.

Chapter 3

"Right now, you couldn't light this forest on fire with a blow torch!"

The key, we learned, is pine pitch and dry pine needle tinder found at the base of big trees.

"And keep those matches dry!"

This advice came in handy later on. During an overnight excursion with two other companions, the ground deep in snow, we spent a feverish twilight hour collecting a sticky pile of pitch and soggy pine needles. (After that we bagged these precious commodities in a plastic Ziplock and carried it everywhere.) With a lot of sweat and a bit of sorcery, we got the cooking fire going just before dark.

The legend, Paul Petzoldt, in conference

The long shakedown period allowed time for debating the finer points of wilderness ethics. During one of these group talks, one staff member stated unequivocally, "It's totally irresponsible to hike in the wilderness alone. A rescue puts many other lives in danger for your selfishness."

I seemed to be the only one in disagreement. Two summers before I had spent two glorious weeks alone in the High Sierra, hiking from Sequoia National Park to Mineral King, and climbing two high peaks in the process. On one of those summits, Eagle Scout Peak, I chose an exposed class four ridge to the top. I was quickly finding odds with most of the students and some guides. Almost all the students but me had severely limited outdoor experience, but on the other hand most had careers in teaching, counseling, or guidance already.

There were other things I didn't stomach well. A big part of the training was learning to cook large group meals, half of which went uneaten and were surreptitiously buried. The waste bothered me. Paul taught us his famous climbing signals that have become the industry standard, but this stuff was already second nature for me. I was getting frustrated. I had told Paul of my aspirations and expected to climb hard. Though I liked Paul and never lost my affection for him, he had misrepresented the program to me.

Our primary leader was Paul's protégé, whom he'd found while visiting New York City. Jeff had no wilderness experience. As Paul unabashedly told us, he wanted to show that he could groom anyone into a wilderness leader. Jeff took on the role with relish, hoping to please his mentor. Jeff's style, borrowed perhaps from military experience, meant you dropped and did twenty pushups if you were a minute late for the 8 AM daily briefing. I found this kind of junior high school hazing out of place. And it was obvious while demonstrating what to do on a simple climb, as his legs shook uncontrollably, that he didn't have any climbing experience to speak of. The instructor needed instructing.

After ten days my instincts told me emphatically that the program was not for me. As long as I was out here I could travel anywhere—Montana, Canada, places I'd never seen. I let the leaders know my plans and hoped they'd prorate a refund after I left. But soon a senior assistant came by my campsite with a personal plea, promising the second part of the course would involve high-altitude snow and rock climbing and that I'd be much happier. I was no quitter, so I stayed. But the doubts remained.

One of the only things making this outing enjoyable was my tent mate, Natalie. She was from Boise, Idaho, six years younger than me, sweet, on the quiet side, and only one of two people I could commiserate with. Her outside softness was balanced by an inner toughness. She went on to be a leader in the outdoor field as a river guide and guidebook writer. We were glad to have each other as pals.

Day 11. It was snowing outside the tent, hard, a day to hunker down and wait the weather out. But our shakedown period was over and we were scheduled to move on. Natalie came back with news—we were breaking camp. Incredulous, I learned we were going to higher ground, leaving the relative comfort and safety of the forest for the summit of Table Mountain, 11,000-feet high. It is due west of the Grand Teton/Middle Teton col and a notorious wind tunnel. Here, outdoor equipment manufacturers have tested tent prototypes where they hope they don't disintegrate in winds commonly exceeding hurricane force.

Grand and Middle Tetons from Table Mountain

We trudged through wet snow for hours, gaining elevation and losing warmth. My leather boots were pre-Gore-Tex and the beeswax-based Snow Seal applied to boots for waterproofing was not working. Boots and socks were soaked. My pack was back to 75 pounds, a little over half my body weight, with the food needed for the following twenty days. Winds were about forty miles per hour at camp as I flopped into our tent, hands and feet painfully cold. Even in my Alaskan down bag, it took an hour to warm up. The difference between the cold clime-adjusted Easterners and the Californians became obvious as my counterparts had a snowball fight in freezing temperatures. *Learn this lesson well: Cold is your Achilles Heel.* Though I had previously survived freezing nights without shelter—in fact, one of them just below the summit of the Grand Teton only three years before—I would never purposely court such conditions.

Typical Teton weather for June continued for another ten days. Our heavy-duty wool pants and shirts were our best friends. One morning, nature called suddenly and I was five minutes late for 8 AM reveille. Jeff called me out in front of everyone.

"What's your excuse, Stanton?"

"Okay to take a shit, Jeff, or do I need special permission for that?"

A few days later he was twenty minutes late but offered no explanation or apology. No one commented on this lapse, not even in jest.

The group had some mishaps. Someone fell off a steep, loose trail and tumbled thirty feet. The heavy backpack saved him from all but a bruise. Natalie came back one night with news that Susan, an upbeat, good-looking woman from New York whom I had befriended earlier in the trip, was now taking up with Jeff. I groaned my disappointment in her judgment. A couple of days later Natalie's news was worse—on Jeff's advice Susan had eaten a native wild plant and vomited all night.

Chapter 3

After some three weeks of winter, summer arrived with a bang. Snow melted on trails and slopes and rivers rushed silver-white. My mood improved as I broke out my lighter-weight cotton and synthetic clothing, not seen since California. I half-jokingly mused to Natalie if the WEA police would come after me for that. Those who had taken Paul's advice and carried only scratchy wool now suffered in the heat, like English troops in the Revolutionary War. A young assistant chased down a marmot with an ice axe and killed it. He brought it back with great pride and shared it for dinner. I did not partake. With our superabundance of food, I didn't think killing wildlife was called for.

We did some ice axe arrest and easy climbing practice. I was biding my time, suspended in my own purgatory. Were we going to climb peaks or not? The weather had been perfect for a week and a half, yet the promised high-altitude mountaineering was not happening. Finally one night, Jeff announced that teams could form and a chance to climb a peak would come the following day. I partnered with a friend from Los Angeles, the only other person, besides Natalie, with whom I had some rapport. As the big day dawned, we found winter had temporarily returned. It was cold, dreary, and snowing lightly with poor visibility. My partner and I could see the futility and danger of an attempt and bagged it along with most other teams. Only one or two parties left camp. That day turned out to be our only chance for some serious mountaineering. Soon we broke high camp and returned to the low lands.

The final day was spent testing our knowledge of the past five weeks. If you passed you qualified as a certified outdoor instructor and got a badge to prove it. But by then it didn't matter to me. Never had I been so frustrated in a mountain situation, never so unhappy, never had I felt so much time had been wasted. The second part of the test was an evaluation of the course and instructors. Here I could, at last, unleash all my pent-up fury. It came out in a torrent of words, especially my scorn for the lead instructor. Mountains are a place to be free but I felt a prison had been built around me. One by one, the others turned in their papers, but I wrote on and on. The deadline passed and still I scribbled furiously. Finally, with a cramped hand, I handed my papers in after six hours of non-stop writing.

Two weeks later: My sharpened Salewa crampons bit with a satisfying crunch into frost-hardened snow. We were still in shadow and the early morning air at 11,000 feet hit our lungs like cool mint. The summit of Mt. Shasta, over 14,000-feet high, was hours away, but my climbing partner Joanie and I knew we'd make it. We were strong, confident, and happy. I knew who I was up there. Finally, I was doing what I loved.

My memories of WEA were softening. For all its pitfalls the course did one thing very well: it showed me what I didn't want to do. At the age of thirty, I had reached a crossroads: Should I 'live the dream', become a professional guide, and accept the fact that low pay and few benefits would leave me living on a shoestring? Or should I live a more conventional life? A guide must be prepared to carry the heaviest pack, shoulder enormous responsibility, and, even in extremes, carry a client out. That sure wasn't me at a slight 5'9", 145 pounds. A guide must also be a babysitter, they must like doing the same routes over and over, really like showing others his world. I was too independent for that. And when it came down to a dollar and cents exchange, the experience could be tainted. I felt it would turn into just another job.

Within a year I accepted a full time job working for the family vineyard operation in Napa Valley. It was a perfect solution, a situation where I could keep a foot in the conventional world and one in the alternative. Those five weeks in the Tetons shook loose the chaff. Frankly, the eight hundred bucks was a bargain.

A month after the Mt. Shasta ascent, Greg and I stood on the

Chapter 3

summit of Fairview, the largest dome in Tuolomne Meadows. The slide image shows us both wearing white painter pants with huge grins on our faces. We've just climbed our first Grade IV, over a thousand feet of gleaming granite, some of the best in the world. The sun is glinting low across the Meadows with that brilliant Sierra light you can almost inhale as sustenance.

That morning we had been stymied at a small overhang on the third pitch. No guidebook existed for Tuolomne Meadows then, but we had found some route descriptions in a climbing magazine by a well-known guidebook author. His advice would have taken us away from the safety of the main crack and out onto the sheer, hold-less face to circumvent the overhang. No amount of scrutiny revealed holds large enough for the rating, or any holds at all for that matter. We scratched our heads and finally ignored the advice and continued up the straightforward crack. It was a key moment then, realizing the experts can only take you so far. After that, you're on your own. Take what you can from them and move on. It's not all usable.

Greg and I shared a back-slapping hug. Our descent route off the dome's backside was a long sloping decline to the forest. We'd be down before dark but first had a quick dip in the stream to wash off in the last warmth of the sun. We rustled up some rice and beans at the picnic table by Lembert Dome while the sky paled and turned black. We put our night kit together and stumbled into the woods to find the perfect site, no tent, just our down bags to keep us warm under a sky full of white fire. I figured I could live this life just about forever.

Chapter 4
Quest for the Fourteeners

To those who have struggled with them, the mountains reveal beauties they will not disclose to those who make no effort. That is the reward the mountains give to effort. And it is because they have so much to give and give it so lavishly to those who will wrestle with them that [people] love the mountains and go back to them again and again...the mountains reserve their choice gifts for those who stand upon their summits.
—Sir Francis Younghusband

In 1985 I met a new climbing partner at the Consumnes River crags in the Sierra foothills. Mark was a softly spoken, sandy-blond haired guy with a pleasant smile. His husky build allowed him to carry punishing loads. He'd worked as a farrier in the Sierra foothills, based in the little town of Penryn, hauling a hundred-pound anvil in and out of his truck, and shoeing horses for a living. Now as a salesman for Fort Dodge, a veterinary drug company, he drove huge swaths of eastern California and Nevada to make his sales contacts.

If Mark was driving, his passengers had to endure his deplorably bland music tastes, usually some station playing *Musak*, with orchestral versions of 'Eleanor Rigby' and 'We've Only Just Begun'. It was like riding with your parents. I ignored it by anticipating adventures ahead. Mark was invariably pleasant and when he agreed with you, which was often, his succinct, habitual reply was a mild affirmative "that's it". Mark would have fit into Midwestern society seamlessly.

One of the occupational hazards of climbing is the toll it takes on one's hands. After a few years they can take on the gnarled look of a senior citizen. Gloves aren't a good option because one needs to feel the texture of the rock and its nuances to climb safely. Sharp rock or bad climbing technique means cuts and scratches, known as 'gobis' in climbing jargon. Once, to help me heal one of these gobis, Mark pulled a tube of white cream out of his pack sold only for domestic livestock.

"Here, this stuff is better than any over the counter medicine you can buy."

It was indeed.

My desire to climb all peaks over 14,000 feet in California (known as fourteeners) developed in a slow, organic way. I'd topped Mt. Whitney and Mt. Shasta twice each and was fifteen years into a climbing career before the idea took hold. Once I decided to make a quest out of it, I continued in this relaxed manner, enjoying each ascent without feeling compelled to rush.

The whole idea of climbing fourteeners may have been born in Colorado, where there are plenty of opportunities. Coloradans know their mountains. An astounding 500,000 ascents are made each year in the Centennial state, where 53 peaks stand over 14,000 feet high. For Coloradans, it's a rite of passage. In sharp contrast, the word fourteener is not in most Californians' lexicon. The closest we come to a mountain obsession centers on Mt. Whitney (14,505 feet), the highest peak in the lower 48 states. About thirty-thousand climbers a year attempt it but only a third of those will summit. A distant second is Mt. Shasta, with 5,000 successful ascents a year. It's unlikely the average Californian could name any of the other fourteeners in their state.

The biggest factor in this discrepancy may be accessibility. Generally, Colorado peaks have gentle slopes where altitude presents the greatest challenge. In stark contrast, most of the Sierra's highest peaks are technically demanding. This winnows out the hikers from the climbers quickly.

Most of California's fourteeners are in the central and southern

Chapter 4

part of the Sierra Nevada range, but two are outside of it—Mt. Shasta in the southern Cascades and White Mountain in the rain shadow of the Sierra. The epicenter of alpine climbing in the Sierra is the Palisades sub-range west of Big Pine, California, with five fourteeners (or seven, depending on your source). The Palisades are considered the finest alpine climbing in the range and deservedly so. Routes like the U-Notch on North Palisade (14,242 feet) and the Swiss Arete on Mt. Sill (14,162 feet) are lifetime goals for many climbers. The dark metamorphic rock that forms the jagged and serrated topography of the Palisades is more like the Tetons than the majority of this mainly granitic range. And unlike many lower Sierra peaks, they often present no 'easy' side.

Both Mark and I hungered for mountain peaks, so in August 1985 we set aside two weeks in the Palisades, eager to experience the highest and wildest we could find in the state. But then Mark's boss pinned an extra sales trip on him out to Ely, Nevada. I decided on a solo trip for the first week, after which he'd join me for the second.

My new Toyota pickup hummed over Tioga Pass and up to Glacier Lodge, out of Big Pine, without a complaint. Before it burned down, Glacier Lodge was a fine old pine beam structure located at 8,000 feet, where the road ends. They had a store and restaurant and a nearby campground. Glacier Lodge restaurant served the best spare ribs ever. Once, chowing down on these delicious victuals, a chair leg broke out from under me, but I didn't miss a bite. Today, I was too fired up to stop for a meal. I sped up the South Fork of Big Pine Creek trail to Willow Lake, the first real campsite, but pushed on to Brainard Lake, far more beautiful with better proximity to the peaks. Brainard (despite the odd name) is a sapphire gem of a lake set among high, steep walls of rock on three sides. This was my home for the next week.

The next day I rested, watching the sun and shadows play

on the high peaks above, tantalizing me with their beauty. In the morning I rose before dawn, hydrated two packets of instant oatmeal for breakfast, stuffed bagels, cheese, and chocolate into my rucksack, and made sure the crampons and ice axe were secure. For a long day of mountaineering one should start slowly and build up steam, but in my eagerness, I set a blistering pace in my rush for higher ground.

The contour intervals on the Big Pine 15-minute topographic map indicate moderate elevation gain east and south of Brainard Lake. Instead of the shorter but steeper direct route, I took a large loop, first heading east, then south toward the Thumb (13,888 feet) and finally west toward Middle Palisade (14,040 feet). My route took me over frozen snowfields, talus slopes, exquisite high alpine meadows deep in hoar frost, where fresh glacial meltwater gurgled in crazy meanders between grassy banks. In the big cirque bowl west of the Thumb, I was nearly sprinting over easy ground, skirting its small glacier before coming to a halt at the base of the Middle Palisade glacier itself.

Taking the crampons off the pack I carefully placed my boots into each one, threading the leather straps through each metal ring, making sure they were tight without cutting off circulation. My ice axe was the same wooden-handled, five-dollar special the Sierra Club provided for their Basic Mountaineering Training Course in 1968. Just at that point, the sun poked its welcome rays over Southfork Pass. Far below on a flat shelf, among a world of tumbled boulders, people were stirring from their tents, a site far above my own camp, placed to facilitate their summit day.

The glacier looked steep as it ascended several hundred feet to the mountain's rocky base. I placed each foot with great care on the frozen snow, left hand gripping the ice axe head, right hand on the shaft, ready to arrest in case of a fall, as I traversed up and right. After a while, I found a rhythm, became more confident and soon the glacier ended. Here I placed my ice tools in

Chapter 4

a rock niche and continued up and right in a prominent rock gully, now moving much faster, being more at home on this terrain.

A third of the way up the face this easy gully ended abruptly, and I looked down a highly exposed northeast face. Above, the wall steepened in a series of short steps and ledges, the latter littered with large and small stones. I was pleased to be climbing alone at this time because a stone accidentally kicked loose by climbers above could have been injurious or fatal. I climbed carefully over this high-angle minefield, boulders ready to launch like a cannon shot.

The sun warmed the rock and I climbed faster. Near the top, the ledges ended and the rock was more solid. Tenzing Norgay, Sir Edmund Hillary's partner on the first ascent of Everest, remarked in his autobiography *Tiger of the Snows*, that whenever he neared a summit his 'third lung' would kick in. It's a great metaphor, one that I've felt many times in the form of increased desire, power, and confidence. That's how I finished the climb on Middle Palisade, with a burst of energy. I surmounted the ridge crest and moved left a few feet to the actual summit. The great Palisade crest running eight miles from Bishop Pass to South Fork Pass is like a jagged row of shark teeth upon which I balanced like a mote of dust on one of these higher incisors. To the north was Norman Clyde Peak, then the massive bulwark of Mt. Sill, followed by North Palisade, Thunderbolt Peak, and Mts. Winchell and Agassiz. To the south was Disappointment Peak, the Thumb, and much farther was Split Mountain, once known as the Southeast Palisade. Four of these peaks are over 14,000, the rest well over 13,000 feet above sea level.

With an hour and a half before noon. I studied the summit register, then added my own entry. These summit register boxes are made of two cast-aluminum, matching sides, fastened by two long-threaded screws. Inside you'll find paper and a pencil. Some climbers scribble out small essays, but generally, people just write their name, hometown, and ascent details. Some entries are entertaining, some boastful, (reached summit from <u>trailhead</u> in 3 hours!), some boring, many are reverent or religious. Sometimes you find your friends, and sometimes you'll see an entry from as long ago as the 1920s. Once I found Jules Eichorn's signature on Lippincott Mountain near Mineral King. Jules, Glen Dawson, and Norman Clyde were the best mountaineers in California in the 1920s and '30s. It's not uncommon to see the names of more modern mountaineers, like the peripatetic Galen Rowell or Peter Croft.

I had a leisurely lunch surveying the kingdom. Then I secured the register, placing it under some summit stones, where it would be safe from thunder and lightning storms and the heavy snows of winter.

Halfway down the face, I encountered the party seen stirring at their camp hours ago. They were four, in two roped teams, moving steadily but cautiously. They'd been watching me a good part of the morning and were amazed at my pace.

"What did you eat for breakfast today?!"

In those youthful days at high altitude, it often felt like I could live on nothing but air and sunshine.

Over the years I've found a relationship between party size and speed, often the larger the group, the slower it moves. Speed can be a good thing in the mountains when afternoon thunderstorms strike the high peaks. But speed is only one advantage of going alone. One can find the perfect rhythm not available when hiking with a partner. Naturally, there is a big price to pay when things go wrong. The mountain gods have been good to me in my years of solo hiking and climbing.

In the notes section of Rene Daumal's unfinished book *Mt. Analogue: A Novel of Symbolically Authentic, Non-Euclidean Adventures in Mountain Climbing* is a quote:

> *You cannot stay on the summit forever, you have to come down*

Chapter 4

again. So why bother in the first place? Just this: what is above knows what is below, but what is below does not know what is above.

Besides the metaphorical implications, there was a plain and practical truth in this statement. From the summit of Middle Palisade, I had seen my looping approach was almost whimsical. To descend to camp, a much more direct route was desirable. At the mountain's base, I strapped the crampons to the rucksack and grabbed the ice axe, sinking my boots, heel first into the now soft snow, and plunge-stepped north to Finger Lake.

Standing on the rim above this gorgeous, fjord-like, electric blue body of water, I marveled for many minutes at its beauty. A foray around the west end of the lake ended in an impasse and now tired, I retraced my steps to the east side, where a narrow use trail, perched between the water and land, barely admitting passage. Arriving at camp, I flopped down on my sleeping pad and didn't move until dinner, listening to the wind in the pines and the lapping waters of the lake, feeling the kind of contentment only to be found after a day in the mountains like this.

Two days later I was heading toward South Fork Pass again with the thought of climbing the Thumb (13,388 feet). From the small glacier at its base, its complex mass of black rock walls was daunting. Besides, it was pleasure enough to mountain travel without a goal. I decided to give up on the idea of peak climbing. Talus slopes gave way to a final steep scree slope where a series of small, closely spaced rock falls rained down. They came out of the mouth of a small gully near the top. I watched this process for some time then decided it did not present a serious danger. From South Fork Pass was a vista of the vast alpine desert surrounding Mather Pass on the John Muir Trail. Just north of that was the Golden Staircase, the last section of trail to be built in 1938. Our Explorer Scout group had passed through there during my first summer in the Sierra, back when I was an impressionable fifteen years of age.

I spent a leisurely hour lunching before returning, timing my descent to pass the scree flows without harm. On the talus boulders below, I met two fit young men carrying large packs. One of them was wearing a pair of small boots I would characterize as gym shoes in those days.

"Don't you worry about turning an ankle wearing those things?" I asked.

I still wore Pivetta leather hiking boots that weighed over two pounds apiece. They were capable of pounding down thousands of feet of scree slope with impunity like I'd done on the Great Kaweah a few years back. They were genuine mountaineering boots with a stiff ridge running around the entire boot to hold crampons securely.

"Nope" he grinned, "I'm just real careful where I step each time. These babies weigh three times less than yours," nodding at my shit kickers. "Over the course of a day, your leg muscles are lifting thousands of pounds of boot. I'm far less fatigued at the end of the day with these little house slippers."

I had noticed a strain in my upper thighs on occasion at day's end.

Still, I shook my head in disbelief but wished him well and walked off in wonderment. Little did I know I'd just seen the wave of the future—the era of the light hiker boot was dawning. In my bachelor days, my walk-in closet at home was a virtual mountaineering museum, holding my prized Pivetta Muir Trails, a mid-sized boot I wore for fifteen trouble-free years. Just like everyone else now, I wear light hikers for day hiking and backpacking that wear out after one season and get thrown away. None of them make the museum rack.

The snowfields, firm in the early morning, had a patina of soft crust over them on the return, perfect for boot skiing. In boot skiing, you look for moderate slopes and good runouts at the bottom with no limb-cracking boulder fields. Leg muscles get a stronger workout than on skis. With axe in arrest position, I let gravity do the work, sometimes lurching in patches of sticky snow. It takes some good balance. I sailed down three snow slopes this way and arrived at camp midday.

The next morning, I left what had come to feel like home, and in my usual way, thanked the ground for six nights of restful sleep. Then, for good measure, I thanked the mountains for their counsel and the lake for peace. Back at Glacier Lodge by mid-morning, Mark was already there to greet me, packed and eager to get on the North Fork trail. My careful preparations meant a trip to town was unnecessary. A food cache for this second week (in those days no bears lived on the east side, therefore no need for bear lockers) awaited in my car. It went into my Dana backpack along with more climbing gear.

Hefting my pack, I immediately felt the extra weight. Besides the ice axe and crampons, we now had 150 feet of nylon climbing rope, aluminum carabiners, slings, and camming and wedging devices called Friends and stoppers. The rope was heaviest, and Mark volunteered to carry it. Having Mark along was like having my own trekking porter.

The North Fork of Big Pine Creek trail climbs steeply to First Falls, where we stood on a footbridge enjoying the cooling effect of the roaring and frothy snowmelt beneath us. Orange and maroon Leopard Lilies on long stalks waved in the breeze created by the windy tumult. Only a few steps took us away from this riparian oasis and we were abruptly thrown back into the dry, sage-covered hillsides. The enormous bulk of Mt. Alice (11,630 feet) squats to the west like a gigantic pile of bear scat. It is uniformly and easily sloped to the summit, presenting no challenge or interest to a mountaineer. Steve Roper in his *Climbers Guide to the High Sierra* called it, "One of the ugliest mountains in the Sierra, a veritable pile of rubble."

When the trail leveled off, Jeffrey pines appeared like solitary sentinels. The landscape changed dramatically as we entered the whimsically named Cienega Mirth. Cienega is a Spanish word meaning, "a wet, marshy area where groundwater bubbles to the surface." Trees provided dotted shade in this park-like area and a stream bubbled through the lush ground cover of mountain azalea and brightly colored flowers like Tiger Lily, Columbine, and Gentian.

Near here is the fortress-like Lon Chaney cabin, built of granite and lodgepole pine beams, still in excellent condition. The former horror picture movie star loved to fly fish on this stream more than anything else in his life. The cabin was designed by famous Los Angeles architect Paul Revere Williams in 1929–30. Chaney was to enjoy the cabin only a few months before his death at the age of 47. The cabin, on the National Register of Historic Places, is kept locked by the Forest Service and still used as a backcountry ranger station.

Where the canyon narrows and a waterfall gushes out of a slot, you leave the chaparral behind for good. A shady pine forest, cooler air, and we started getting excited about catching glimpses of the high peaks. An enormous mass of boulders and dirt appeared on the left, a moraine left by receding glaciers in the last ice age. Trees populated this agglomeration. Suddenly I stopped in my tracks.

"Mark, I've been here before, what the hell…?"

This was supposed to be my first trip up the North Fork. But like faces (but not like names), I never forget a landscape. After a second it dawned on me that this was the site of the Sierra Club's Basic Mountaineering Training Course weekend in the spring of 1968. Up there, while digging out a snow cave, I'd taken a blow to my shin when the ice axe slipped. A week later the wound infected and turned to blood poisoning. I'd have to be more careful this time.

Chapter 4

The gothic cathedral of Temple Crag, Palisades, Sierra Nevada

There are seven gorgeous lakes on the North Fork, but whoever 'named' them had an appalling lack of imagination. They are simply numbered one through seven in order of approach. But Temple Crag, towering over Third Lake, is well-named, a Gothic church of a mountain, one foot short of 13,000 feet. Our camp at Third Lake has heart palpitating views of Temple Crag. The massive center prow or north buttress of Temple Crag, soaring two-thousand feet above the talus slopes, holds Dark Star, the longest route in the Palisades. On either side of the north buttress are a galaxy of pinnacles and gullies, turrets and gargoyles, flying buttresses, and vertical box canyons. You could easily spend a day admiring this great peak, watching shadow and light play follow the leader across its amazing bulk. On its northeast side are popular routes like Moon Goddess Arete and Venusian Blind Arete. On the north-east shoulder is Contact Pass, the easiest route to the summit.

Though it wasn't in the original plan, Mark and I decided we had to climb this monarch of a mountain. We searched for a weakness in the mountain, finding it in the North Chute—a long, continuous gully whose mouth spills onto a massive talus cone. Though much of the upper route was hidden, it seemed to lead by labyrinthine ways to the ridge west of the summit, where an easy climb led to the summit. We had no route description of this climb and would be relying instead on our instincts.

We slept late, until well after sunrise. In our daypacks went only cheese, crackers, pemmican bars, and water. We figured the route was third class and left the rope in camp. A steep, loose scree slope flowed out of the mouth of the great gully entrance shaped like a beard, punctuated by a scrim of snow curling out of the mouth like spittle. The gully yawned open and we stepped Jonah-like into the whale's jaws. The going was straightforward class 2 until pinching down to a bottleneck, blocked by a massive boulder. Turning it on the left was impossible and on the right it overhung. Clearly, this was a spot for a rope. Second thoughts didn't help, so with Mark spotting me I got up into an alcove and turned a small roof, found a secure spot, and dropped one end of a long sling. Mark used it for an extra handhold, and we continued on easier ground to the summit ridge.

Just as we thought, it was an easy scramble to the 12,999-foot summit. The register hidden under summit rocks had entries going back to 1941. For July of 1970 was the entry 'viento esamo', left by my high school friends David and Mercy Russel who had been guided up Moon Goddess Arete by the venerable guide and philosopher, Doug Robinson. Leaving, we leaped a narrow cleft that acted like a gunsight, with a view thousands of feet down to our tent near Third Lake. Loose rocks led to the fourth-class gully above Contact Pass. Once again, a rope wouldn't have hurt here. We down-climbed facing out then turned inwards as it got steeper, paying close attention to every hold. With elation, we finished the pitch and the technical problems were over. (On another, roped, unsuccessful attempt of Temple Crag ten years later via Contact Pass, I was surprised by the difficulty and exposure of this crux pitch.) Emboldened by our success, we made preparations for the culminating climb of the trip,

Chapter 4

the U-Notch on North Palisade.

Only a half-mile from our camp lay the well-worn trail to Sam Mack Meadow and Palisade glacier. But with youthful vigor, we decided to hump our heavy loads up a promising talus gully that seemed to lead directly to our objective. The going was slow and ponderous and took us a good half-day but rewarded us with a level patch of dry ground below the glacier with front-row views of the Palisades Crest. To our left was Mt. Gayley, detached from the crest and lower by about 500 feet. To its right, the awesome bulwark of Mt. Sill and the sweeping curve of the Swiss Arete, prominent from Hwy 395 north of Big Pine. Farther right was the U-Notch, a snow vein leading straight to the crest east of North Palisade, its distinctive northeast wall a snowy chest topped by an arrow tip summit.

The sun was setting but still warm, softening the snow of the second largest glacier in California. Later, pink alpenglow caught the peaks on fire, and we sought the warmth of our tent as the thermometer swiftly plummeted. The glacier would freeze solid overnight. Despite our excitement, tinged with anxiety about the morrow, we slept soundly after our tough approach hike.

Mark's digital watch alarm woke us at 4 AM. All around was unremitting silence. All the little streams and rivulets that awaken during the day were still, frozen hard. Even the wind was mute. Desire overcame lethargy as we dressed inside our down bags. A water bottle accidentally left outside the tent was frozen. Fortunately, we'd placed our boots inside our bags. After an appropriately aimed pee, we fired up the Optimus stove for oatmeal and hot chocolate. The leather straps on the crampons, which had been left outside, were frozen stiff and difficult to lace. The glacier began just west of our tent. Rucksack on, axe in hand, I was ready.

"Shall we?" Mark had been ready for five minutes.

"We're off!" I said gleefully.

North Palisade peak and glacier from Mt. Gayley

The dream of climbing the U-Notch had been hatched seven years back while working in a mountaineering store in the Santa Barbara suburb of Goleta. After a summer of travel, I was broke, jobless, and homeless. Each night I parked my truck in a turnout across from Scofield Park in the foothills. It was the coolest crash pad in the county—quiet, a burbling stream for accompaniment, the scent of rock rose blooming on the nearby sandstone bridge, and best of all, free. I came in late and left early, and no one disturbed me. I went down to the gym at Santa Barbara City College for a free shower most mornings, or just jumped in the creek. I lived this way for a month until finding the job. After two weeks, my first paycheck arrived and I could afford to rent a room in Goleta.

I was new at retail sales and did my best to preserve my lowly position as a sales clerk. Only three weeks into the job, the head sales manager, Sid, left me as the sole sales clerk for five days while he went on a climbing trip. He returned with tales of bad weather, hard ice, and a failed attempt on North Palisade via the U-Notch. The next day I reported for work and was informed by the boss my employment was over. I was never told

Chapter 4

why. Sid was already giving the new guy the orientation talk. Though not my main motivation, a petty, less commendable part of me wanted success on this climb as some kind of weird retribution. Sid had come off as a mountaineer of some experience and ability and he had turned back. I wasn't going to turn back if I could help it.

Our crampons bit noisily into the firm snow, making ten finely etched holes punctuated by a larger dot of the ice axe. The Palisades glaciers have few crevasses, and we made steady uphill progress, the rope still in the rucksack. Dawn light rose around us like a curtain revealing actors on a glacial stage. Black massifs presented themselves shyly at first, then more boldly with fiery pink and orange hues. The sun did not find us before we reached the mountain's base and our first great obstacle, the bergschrund. Here, the glacier pulls away from the rock with a twenty-foot gaping fissure. The upper wall of this bergshrund reminded me of geology class lessons in slip faults. It was sheer to overhanging in most places, beyond our skill level and equipment capacity. Only in one place to the far right was there a break in its defenses. There, a jumbled, concaving bridge of rotten snow descended into the bergshrund and then climbed back out onto the 40-degree couloir that shot 700 feet to the U-Notch above. It looked horribly unreliable. There was no question that here we would rope up.

Below the snow bridge, the great maw of the bergshrund went down into the icy depths an unknown distance. A cold and inhuman breath rose up from it. For the first time this trip I grew fearful, shivering from cold and fear. My gut clenched up. Suddenly I wondered if we could do this. But Mark was eager to go so I sank my axe deep, with the belay rope looped around the head, then put my boot on top and told Mark he was on belay. Mark weighs a good 190 pounds, so I prayed the belay would hold in case the bridge collapsed. My partner carefully straddled the narrow bridge until he was safely across and set up his own belay at the bottom of the couloir. Surprisingly, it was easier than it looked and soon I was across.

My lead. The angle was steeper than anything I'd done in my short snow and ice career. The old Salewa crampons bit well but the pick of my axe couldn't find a purchase in the snow, frozen almost hard as ice. I stayed close as possible to the right wall and occasionally placed a stopper or hex in the rock, but ice screws were not in the arsenal. At one point I was 50 feet beyond my last protection point. With no possibility of an ice axe arrest, a fall would be disastrous, so I narrowed my focus to each step. With great relief, a decent belay appeared as the rope ran out.

But now the angle increased for Mark, who also found scant protection. When he was 40 feet out without a single gear placement, the fear, like a fist in the gut, returned. It's always worse on belay—at least on lead you can move or plan some move. We were both shocked at the hardness of the snow, though with more experience we'd have known that by August these conditions were common. I kept silent, though the thought of a leader fall and failed belay would mean a swift trip into the freezer locker below us. I didn't fancy such an ending.

Slowly, Mark led on. After an eternity came the call of off belay and a flood of relief washed over me. I quickly closed the distance between us and saw the angle had lessened above. My confidence surged as I took over the lead. The sun was now in the couloir and snow began to soften, at first only a few crystals on the surface, then enough for my axe to bite. The slope angle continued to lessen and we moved faster, our fears now forgotten. The couloir veered right, then ended and we stashed our axes and crampons in a small alcove. Our second major obstacle out of the way, we now came to two easy fifth class chimneys. This kind of ground was familiar, and I surged up the first pitch hardly bothering with protection. Mark wanted me to lead the second chimney and I didn't waste a second thinking about it. We had been swapping leads all the way, but it didn't occur to

Chapter 4

me something might be amiss.

At the top of the second chimney, I noticed Mark was perceptibly slowing down. Unsure of which way to go, I turned left but quickly realized it was a dead end. Returning, I blurted out:

"It's gotta be up this way Mark, we can't be far now!" I was on fire with summit fever.

But then I looked at Mark and knew something was wrong. The spirit was gone from his eyes and his breathing had a strange, labored quality to it.

"I'm gonna stay here Ken, my breathing is off. Can't get enough air."

"You sure!?"

I was completely baffled. We were only about 300 feet from the top.

'Yeah, go on, I'll be okay here," and I knew he would be. He'd already taken the pack off and put his back against the rock.

"I'll be okay," he repeated.

I hesitated, then took off at a fast pace. The arête rose at a steep, steady angle to the classic triangular summit. The way was narrow, exposed, with stupendous views thousands of feet down either side. I was feeling my oats and that 'third lung' had kicked in. There were massive boulders to clamber over, beside, or underneath, their skin a rough, satisfying texture. Finally, there was only the sparkling blue canopy of sky above me. To the north, south, and west all that could be seen were oceans of mountain peaks. To the east, the big trench of the Owens Valley ten thousand feet below, the White Mountains almost as high as the Sierra and the Basin and Range of Nevada beyond. As I stood on the topmost point, I felt a wonderful, enlivening lightness of body, as if I had alighted from above rather than struggled up from below.

Norman Clyde, who made several thousand ascents in this range, loved this mountain. He climbed it thirty-five times and now I could understand why. Both he and mountain rambler

Smoke Blanchard agreed that this is the greatest summit in the Sierra. For me, it would be my only ascent. But I doubt whether Clyde could remember each of his ascents as well as I remember this one. I thought of Mark and wished he could be here. I couldn't have made it without him. Hell, I'd nearly backed off twice in fear. How is one to know when to push on and when to retreat? When to be bold and when to be prudent? What separates success from failure, triumph from tragedy? Sometimes these decisions are not made but simply happen. I stood on the summit through grace and luck, thankful, knowing it could just as easily have been me, laboring for breath 300 feet below.

The elation one can feel on a summit must be tempered on the way down. Many accidents happen on the descent when one is tired and not paying strict attention to changing conditions. Reluctantly, I turned back after a half-hour and descended the ridge. Mark was there with a wan smile and congratulations and we rappelled the two chimneys, retrieving our axes and crampons. The crampons we tied to our rucksacks because, to our great delight, direct sun in the couloir had transformed the rock-hard snow into perfect plunge step material. Each step created its own foothold so secure a fall probably could have been arrested without an ice axe. Nevertheless, we took care not to be overconfident. At the bergshrund, we cautiously stopped well before the lip, unfurled the rope, and tied in. The late afternoon light allowed us to peer further into the gaping maw, the terrifyingly beautiful blue/white ice far below. The snow bridge was softer now and we padded across like cats holding our breath. Then all the dangers were passed. We had seen no one all day, nor heard any voices and I considered that a blessing. The experience had been all ours.

While Mark plodded carefully along, I skittered playfully down the glacier with the late afternoon sun warm on our backs. A feeling of utter bliss washed over me and once again that feeling of lightness returned as if I was floating just above the glacier's surface.

Only later that evening as we prepared for sleep did I properly listen to Mark's short, wheezing breaths and the lightbulb finally went on. Mark had bravely downplayed his condition—what an idiot I'd been not to understand. I'd read many accounts of pulmonary edema but hadn't been in the presence of someone suffering from it. All those accounts took place in higher mountains, the Himalaya, the Andes, or Denali. Pulmonary edema can occur anywhere above 10,000 feet, but with Mark being the fit mountaineer he was, it just hadn't registered.

Darkness was complete and we were situated at the head of a thousand-foot talus gully perhaps un-negotiable even with headlamps.

"Mark, do you think we should try to descend tonight?"

"No, it's impossible. I'll be okay tonight and we'll get it tomorrow," he replied almost casually.

His calm demeanor took some of my anxiety away. But as I listened into the night to his ragged, rattling half breaths, I couldn't help but wonder. How long could this condition go on before it's fatal? The answer eluded me. Sleep came not knowing what I'd wake to.

In the morning Mark was still chipper, upbeat through his wheezing. I pleaded with him to leave his pack and descend unburdened, but he wouldn't have any of it.

"It's no problem, we're going downhill now."

We picked our way slowly down the rocky gully and by Third Lake his breathing had eased. A surprisingly quick descent to the trailhead was accomplished. By the time we had driven to Owens Valley his breathing had returned to normal.

"Don't you want to see a doctor in town?" I asked incredulously.

"Nah, I'm feeling good now. I'll see a doctor at home."

Mark and I parted ways. A week later, I called and asked if he had seen his doctor but he said no, what for? He was back to normal. Mark had the right stuff for a mountaineer. Within the year he went to climb Alaska's Denali and after a thirty-day training period, topped the 20,000-foot peak via the Cassin route, one of the peak's most serious endeavors. No sign of pulmonary edema appeared.

As for my return, the wine grape harvest was already underway. It was a shocking transition. After two weeks in the purity of the high mountain air where temperatures never exceeded 80° F, I was cast into the over-oxygenated, dust-laden, searing heat of Napa Valley where temperatures often exceed 100° F for days on end. In the morning I reported for work at 6 AM. For the next two months, my main sustenance would be memories of mountains past and dreams of those to come.

After North Pal, I continued to pursue my dream of climbing all of California's fourteeners. But I wanted to make each one special, each a memorable, unforgettable experience. And so I took my time, usually climbing one or two a year, solo or with friends, every one distinct in my memory. Mts. Williamson and Tyndall have the epic approach up Shepard Pass, six thousand feet of ascent in six miles just to achieve the base of these mountains. Both were done solo. Mt. Russel was also climbed solo, with a view north to the 'Crater Lake of the Sierra', the amazing Tulainyo Lake, highest in the range, like a cerulean jewel in the lotus. Robin and I climbed Split Mountain and then, a few days later, Thunderbolt Peak. It requires an exposed, gymnastic, and strenuous lieback of twenty feet with no protection to surmount the summit block. The summit register is bolted to its side to keep climbers honest. We were chased off the top by a quick-moving storm that dumped rain and hail on us lower down. White Mountain was done in late October when the thermometer dropped to 12° F above zero on the summit. My last fourteener in 1994 was Mt. Langley, an easy stroll over broad scree slopes.

During the time I was finishing my quest, Porcella and Burns published California's Fourteeners. *In the book, they*

Chapter 4

included two more peaks, Starlight and Polemonium, both in the Palisades. They cite popular usage but no technical evidence for inclusion as fourteeners. In certain mountaineering circles these days, controversy swirls around how a fourteener is defined, in fact how any mountain should be called a mountain. In the absurd extreme, every bump on a massif with multiple high points could be called a separate mountain. Colorado has somewhat arbitrarily solved the issue by declaring that a mountain must be separated from other high points by a saddle of at least 300 feet. By this definition, neither Polemonium nor Starlight are peaks, only high points on a ridge. But this also excludes Mt. Muir and Thunderbolt Peak, the latter, ascended in 1931, considered the last fourteener to be climbed in California. When I began my quest, our state had 13 peaks over the 14,000-feet. mark; with the Burns/Porcella book it went to 15. If the Colorado definition is adopted by California, that number would go down to 11. All that being said, these are arcane issues and ultimately of no lasting importance. Mountains rise and mountains fall with geologic activity as well as with improved measuring techniques. If 'doing' the fourteeners gets people off the couch, well and fine, but hopefully in the process, they will benefit from the more lasting pleasures and rewards, and character-building values that mountaineering brings.

Chapter 5
Steve

The reward of a thing well done, is having done it.
 —Ralph Waldo Emerson

The man at the pumice mine didn't seem to mind we had just driven onto the grounds without permission. He was willing to show us the way through. We followed his pickup truck past tumbledown old buildings and ratty wire fences until he stopped abruptly.

"There," he pointed.

In front of us was a high, steep hill, consisting of loose hummocky dirt and jumbled boulders. There was no road that I could see or even a faint track.

"There?" I said, crinkling up my face perplexed.

"That's a four-wheel drive, ain't it? Right over that hill is your connecting road to the trailhead."

"Thanks," I said, unsure if I meant it.

"No problem." He hurried back to work in a cloud of white dust.

I put the Nissan into 4 low and crawled uphill at a 30-degree angle like I'd done it before. The truck wove its way between some boulders and lurched over others. Halfway up Steve got out to scout a gully we'd have to cross at a diagonal. It seemed a perfect scenario for a tip over. But the mine employee had been so confident like he'd directed dozens of other trailhead seekers this way. Steve let me drive the gully alone (not as bad as it looked) and then we bounced and scraped up to the top where we found the McMurray Meadows Road. It was a minefield of boulders but more or less level.

Red Lake trailhead had intrigued me in the recent past, with its remoteness, difficulty of access, and two unsuccessful attempts to find it. Now, finally here, on a brilliantly clear day in the fall of 1987, the trailhead was empty and showed little use. There was a simple turnaround, a tent site or two on bare earth, and a Forest Service display case, with general information on backcountry use but nothing on the Red Lake trail. We hoped to camp at Red Lake at the base of Split Mountain, one of California's 14,000-foot peaks. Making our best guess, we followed a use trail into a rocky canyon. The trail gradually disappeared but we hiked on into this seldom-used canyon, sweating our way up steep boulder fields and thrashing through willow thickets ablaze in the yellow leaves of autumn.

I took a picture of Steve standing next to his backpack on the ground beside him. Behind him is the 'V' of the canyon we've ascended, the volcanic buttes near Big Pine in the Owens Valley, and in the far distance the White Mountains. He strikes a jaunty pose. His left hand is in his pants pocket, his right hand holds a camera lens resting on top of the pack. His gaze, which is away from the camera slightly, seems to be saying, "We may be lost but so what? Here we are so enjoy it already." That was Steve. We hurried on until dusk, finding a level site with an ancient campfire ring and discarded vintage tin cans from the 1950s.

We spent our days exploring this unheralded little canyon, our late afternoons and evenings hunched around a blazing fire. Come 3 PM, when the sun disappeared behind dark vertical walls of granite to the west, the temperature would instantly plunge by 20° F. By dawn, 15° F of frost had left ice on our bags. Mornings we built the fire again to chase the chill until the sun reappeared in the east. One day we climbed to a ridgetop, teetering on cascades of loose scree and talus to see if Split Mountain could be climbed from this direction. But from our high point, we saw that the peak was cut off by jumbled, wild, and

Chapter 5

convoluted country. It didn't take long for us to decide. We turned around and 'boot-skied' down the loose scree slopes to camp in a fraction of the ascent time.

That afternoon we gathered another huge pile of Whitebark pine and ceremonially lit the fire as the sun sank. We talked about mutual interests, women and relationships, the outdoors, spirituality, and when we were out of words, the fire was our entertainment. Steve was a professional photographer and I was hoping to write. That night we made a pact to collaborate on magazine articles about the outdoors. He'd photograph, I'd write, and we'd get them published in Mountain Gazette, or maybe even Conde Nast. It was exciting to think about. When the fire was still a furnace of red-hot coals, we slipped quickly into our down bags open to the night air, the atmosphere so clear, the stars barely glittered and appeared like planets, emitting a steady pure light. I find this kind of darkness, silence, and emptiness oddly comforting. That night the voice of deep silence seemed to connect us with the planets and stars beyond.

Our return next day took only two hours. From the trailhead, we noticed something we'd missed earlier. Just to the north of our lost canyon, a faint line etched its way across a sandy hillside. Chagrined, we recognized the Red Lake Trail and agreed a return at a later date was mandatory. I did get there a few years later, but for Steve, it was not in the cards.

A few years before that outing, I had joined an interleague softball team in St. Helena. The sport had become wildly popular in my town. There were three leagues—men's, older men's (over 40), and coed. Our men's team was nicknamed the Zanzibar Ducks and we had various sponsors over the years: Conn Valley Vineyards, The Spot (a pizza joint), and French Laundry, a famous restaurant in Yountville where you needed to reserve a dinner two months out. It wasn't long after I'd joined the team that Steve showed up—we needed a catcher so that's where we put him. It was the perfect position for Steve. He wasn't a great athlete but with his enthusiasm and directorial skills, he would encourage and exhort us from behind the plate. He was a real team player and, in a way, became the soul of the Ducks.

Our team was comically bad at the beginning, but at least we had fun. Nate would yell from the bench "Ducks on the pond!" whenever we had a base runner. Bob the manager, deep-voiced and calm would step to the plate and clean his bat against his baseball pants by drawing it through his legs at crotch level. His wife Sheila was the vocal powerhouse in the stands, "Come on Bob, **HIT IT!**" with a voice the nearby neighbors could hear behind closed doors.

Steve and I soon became friends on and off the baseball diamond. He worked at Sterling Vineyards part-time and photographed weddings on weekends. He always had lots of friends, both male and female, he had the Italian love for cooking and enjoying life. Once he showed this culinary neophyte an easy way to peel garlic cloves—you just give the clove a twist and the outer skin peels right off. He could eat the spiciest food and on a scale of one to ten, he could handle eleven. He was tall, genial, companionable, and his only annoying trait was his habitual sniffing as if he had allergies or rhinitis. Driving to the mountains we listened to tapes by Ram Dass. Once, after a backpacking trip in the Desolation Wilderness, he confided to me that if karma and reincarnation were true, he'd prefer not to come back to this material life, but rather finish up his work on earth now. Steve thought of himself as an old soul.

During softball season we'd have one practice game and one league game every week. Team spirit was good and we didn't have a problem with practice-game attendance. Main Street Electric was the team to beat. They had a powerhouse line-up of beefy guys who could hit, run and throw and were just plain intimidating. Many of us in the league had played on high school or college baseball teams and were living out carryover dreams of glory. Disputes were common and the league director had a trainload of egos to deal with. Every year we'd finish the season a little higher in the standings but always behind Main Street who invariably won the championship. They were like the Yankees, the team you loved to hate. I would play shortstop and pitch and later moved to third base, where my reflexes could be put to better use. Steve would play first base if Nate was behind the plate. We were still having fun but now we were good too. In 1986 we got to the championship playoff with Main Street but lost. Like the Mets, our cry was "Wait 'till next year!"

By 1987 we were at the top of our game. We kept winning. Bob would hit the long ball, and the rest of us were nickel and diming the pitchers to death. We were hustling down the base paths, stealing bases, playing our hearts out. At season's end, it was Main Street and the Zanzibar Ducks again in the single championship playoff game. Going into that game, we were definite underdogs. We didn't have anything to prove or lose, so we went in loose. It was a low-scoring game. Our fielding was tight and the opposing hitters were getting frustrated. Late in the game, we were ahead by a run, but Main Street rallied. They got a runner on second and then their strongest hitter came to the plate. A wicked line shot down the third base line should have been a game-tying double, maybe even the go-ahead run. I reached out and snagged it right over third base. It was over in a split second while an audible cry of disbelief came from the opposing bench. We held on to the lead for the last inning. The Ducks had actually won! During the traditional end-of-game hand slap ceremony we could see the stunned look on the faces of their players. We were stunned too, but also ecstatic. Happiest of all was Steve, high fiving everyone with a huge silly grin on his face.

Eric, one of our strongest players, was part of the family who owned French Laundry, our sponsor. Years before, they had promised to host the whole team for dinner if we ever won. It was quite a night. Steve took Linda, Bob was with his wife

Sheila, Nate and Cathy were there, Eric and his girlfriend. Afterward, everyone got a homemade award, a softball mounted on a stand with a personal inscription. Mine said something like *the human vacuum cleaner at third base*. I don't think there was ever a prouder team.

In the fall of 1987, Steve, Linda, and I went back to Big Pine and the Eastern Sierra, this time into the heart of the Palisades. We camped at Brainard Lake on the south fork of Big Pine Creek. No one else was there for our mid-October visit. One day we went for a hike toward Southfork Pass and on returning I noticed our descent gully was split in two by a short, intervening ridge that soon joined up below. Linda was already part-way down one side and Steve and I took the other. We told her what we were doing. As the ridge ended, we heard a wailing on the other side from Linda and thought the worst. Steve ran to her, only to find she was unhurt, just frightened to be alone. Steve was like a father, patient and reassuring.

Toward the week's end, we relocated our camp a mile down the trail at Willow Lake. Our goal was to climb Mt. Gayley (13,500 feet), part of the North Palisade glacial cirque. The hike was cross-country after the first mile, an interesting mix of pine forest, talus scrambling, and high alpine meadow strolling. Farther on we had to thread our way through a narrow rock chute followed by an acres-wide-open, glacially polished bowl that led to the peak proper. By this time, Linda, with very little alpine experience, was at the end of her abilities. We had to turn around and both Steve and Linda left for home the next day.

Saying our goodbyes, I repeated the now-familiar terrain. As I came out to the wide granite bowl, an enormous expanse of nearly monotone granitic gray, I spotted a flash of color off to my right under a small overhang. It was a gorgeous, four-pound chunk of pink quartzite, a diamond in the rough. It seemed to be a sign, a portent, so I claimed it as a talisman. Walking it back out to a prominent boulder I placed it on top to retrieve on

Chapter 5

my return.

The summit of Mt. Gayley provided a spectacular view of the North Palisade glacier and the entire cirque. From south to north it was a lineup of heavy hitters—Mt. Sill, then North Palisade, Thunderbolt Peak, Mt. Winchell, and finally Mt. Agassiz. It was October 15, I was in shirt sleeves, and had a birds-eye view of the finest alpine setting in California all to myself. The light off the glacier was a dazzling white, even with sunglasses. I'll have to get Steve up one of these babies next year, I thought. I was incredibly lucky to summit in such perfect weather. (Only two days later on the summit of White Mountain Peak—another fourteener in the White Mountains across the Owens Valley from the Sierra—it was 27° F with a great Pacific storm spilling over the Sierra crest.) I hustled down the trail to my truck and crossed Tioga Pass just before a record snowstorm hit California.

On the descent from Mt. Gayley, I had remembered to place the pink quartzite in my pack and took it home with me. Pink or rose quartz is thought from antiquity to be a stone that speaks to the heart about unconditional love. By chance or, who knows, some mystical influence, I met Susan, my future wife, that same month.

Mount Sill 14,162'

I was mad about the Palisades in those years and returned the following July with Steve to climb Mt. Sill (14,162 feet). Walter Starr Jr., a Sierra vagabond and guidebook writer wrote, "It can be said to be the (ultimate) of all Sierra peaks in the extent and quality of the views it offers."

I'd made an attempt with my sister Leslie years before, crossing Bishop Pass and camping in the Palisade Basin. Our goal was the easy southwest slope. An August snowstorm ruined our chances that first night, and tent-less, we burrowed into the middle of our double-ply plastic tube sheets to wait it out. It was still snowing when we left the next morning.

This time around the weather was clear and warm, much too warm for this elevation. We set up a wonderful camp on a glacier-polished rock slab above Sam Mack Lake with a view of Mt. Sill out our tent door. It was Steve's blue and white striped 'circus tent' with a single pole and no floor, looking very much like a teepee. We lay on top of our down bags at 10 PM, elevation 11,000 feet, with the tent door open and knew they were cooking down in the 'fleshpots' below. I think it was my first awareness that California and by association the world, was going through some radical climate change.

In the morning the snow was soft, so we left our crampons at camp. Most of the north couloir route is class 3 scrambling but one short section is very exposed class 4. It was in shade and some snow was still a bit icy. I had to coax Steve over this and then the summit was ours. Is it the finest summit view in the range as Starr claimed? I can't say, but surely all Palisades summits are spectacular. I was taking my time reading through the summit register when Steve betrayed some anxiety.

"Are we going to be okay going back down?"

"Oh yeah, it won't be any problem at all. In fact, it'll be easier. The sun will be in there and soften up any crusty snow."

We repeated the class four section involving a step around a protruding boulder. A slip here would mean a bad fall. When

Chapter 5

I'd crossed it, I gave Steve a hand, but he didn't need it. He was new to mountaineering, but he handled it with aplomb. Still, I should have carried a short length of rope. When I look back on these exploits decades later I give thanks that no one ever got hurt.

After the 1987 softball season, the Zanzibar Ducks broke up. Steve broke up with Linda (she would refer to him as 'smelly Zanelli' after that) and was going out with Kendall. They got married in 1990 and I was seeing less of him than before. He seemed happily married. By now I was planning to write a book and told my family I'd be taking a year off to do so. On Jan 1, 1991, I began the grand experiment. For four months I did nothing but research and take notes. By April I began to write and by July I was dazzled with the project's scope, drunk with my vision of it. It was working. But even involved in the most satisfying work of my life, I would not abandon my love of climbing. My wife and I had booked two weeks of vacation in Canada for July. We'd fly to Edmonton, meet Robin and Julie and rent a van and see the great parks of British Columbia and Alberta, including climbing in the Bugaboos, a North American equivalent of the Swiss Alps.

On the way to the airport, I got a call. It was from Linda, Steve's old girlfriend. Steve was dead, killed by a drunk driver who smashed into the driver's side of his car after the S turns between St Helena and Calistoga. They were having a wake for Steve the next day, could I attend?

Steve's death hit me hard and has stayed with me all these years. He was 37 at the time, married only a year. We never did collaborate on a magazine article. I think about the photographs he could have made for my book project. The trips we never took. The life he never got to finish. I wish somehow that I could have attended Steve's wake. My book came out in late 1993. On the dedication page is a full-size picture of Steve. He's standing by his backpack in that unheralded little canyon near Red Lake.

On his face is that Mona Lisa smile that seems to say, "Don't worry about me, I'm just fine where I am."

Steve, eastern Sierra

Chapter 6
East Buttress of El Capitan

We are missing some fine climbs by not being light enough to climb clouds.
   —Wade Mills

To be a climber, one has to accept that gratification is rarely immediate.
   —Bernadette McDonald

Now done almost exclusively as a single day free climb, the first ascent of the East Buttress in 1953 took three days and employed aid climbing techniques on several pitches. It was the brainchild of Al Steck, one of America's finest climbers. With him were Bill Long, Will Siri, and Willi Unsoeld who ten years later made the first ascent of Mt. Everest's West Ridge. The East Buttress was the necessary first step to overcoming the daunting defenses of El Cap, before anyone dreamed of scaling its two- and three-thousand-foot vertical to overhanging walls.

Of all the times I've spent on the heights, El Cap's East Buttress stands out in memory as one of my personal favorites. There were so many elements to make it special: great companions, memorable passages on quality granite, high exposure, a descent in the dark which almost necessitated a bivouac, a moonlit return. It is not an especially difficult route and many pass it over for the steeper glories of the most famous cliff in America. But for me, it was a near-perfect adventure.

My first attempt had been made with my friend Mike in early

June of 1990. The climb went well until halfway up when a uniform gray scrim of clouds obscured the sky with a promise of rain. It was a tough decision to descend but the right one. As we drove out of the valley that evening a light rain was soaking the roadway.

On the second attempt, a year later almost to the day, a high-pressure system brought stable, warm weather. Four of us stood in El Cap Meadow admiring the eastern buttress of the Big Stone and noted with admiration how Horsetail Falls, whipped around like a snake charmer's rope by the afternoon winds, occasionally soaked the mid-section of our intended climb. We were to be two rope teams, but Scott's ankle was sore and swollen from a recent fall and that left three: Robin, my capable climbing companion of four years, and Kashi, a new friend of his from Austria. Kashi had climbed only in rock gyms or on sport walls, so he was in for a crash course in traditional climbing in the greatest outdoor gymnasium in the world.

East Buttress of El Capitan

Chapter 6

On the hour-long approach next morning we gawked at storied climbs like Iron Hawk and Zodiac while staying well away from the base with its danger of rockfall and dropped gear. In those days, a plummeting poop bag was a nasty possibility too. The well-trod path led to the far east end of the Captain and the start of our climb. We hurried into our harnesses as another party close behind vied for the same route. I drew the first lead and tied two 9mm ropes to my harness. This is normally a European alpine method, but in a party of three, the leader (either Robin or I) had to simultaneously belay the two below through his belay plate with a bit of sleight-of-hand that takes a while to master. Belaying the two followers one at a time would have been way too slow.

Eagerly, I wiggled up a tight chimney with some strenuous stemming above, stopping in a tiny alcove. A 5.10b face move began Robin's next pitch. It was the technical crux of the entire route, but Robin grabbed a fixed sling and moved on for speed's sake. He then hand-jammed a shallow and narrowly indented slot, his feet on the outside for friction. The belay ledge above was one of Yosemite's notorious red ant ledges. The year before, Mike and I had to perform frenzied dances to keep them off of us. This time there was no sign of the little buggers.

My original inspiration for this climb came from a photograph of Allen Steck on the wonderfully exposed arête pitch from the first ascent in 1953. Now I got to lead it, and though it was easier than I had imagined, it was still quite airy and poorly protected. Robin and I continued on, swapping leads on easy ground, thoroughly enjoying the cooling effect of water droplets from Horsetail Falls on this warmish June day. A small overhang landed us on a flat pedestal, a fine perch half-way up the climb. Here is where Steck and company had bivouacked on the first ascent, and my personal high point from last year. We rested, took stock of things, and had a bite to eat. Above, the wall steepened ominously.

For once I wasn't happy about drawing the lead. It began with a high angle slab featuring a distinctive, central ridge I had to straddle without protection to the main wall. Here the buttress gave only one bold choice—a left diagonal hand crack split a wildly exposed section for 30 to 40 feet, ending in a claustrophobic chimney.

"You don't want this pitch do you, Robin?" I asked half-joking, half-serious.

"It's all yours, Ken, you can do it."

I was having a hard time psyching up, but I wanted the climb badly. Both George Meyers and Don Reid in their guidebooks had made note that this pitch has "many fixed pins" (pitons). There wasn't a single one left now. I made a hack job out of my lead, slugging in cam after cam, hands jamming without precision, feet scrabbling on mostly blank wall. I had to rest on gear once or twice. A fall would have meant a scary swing over the void; I didn't want that option.

Adrenaline surging, I reached the chimney with enormous relief, climbed up an easy crack, and placed four, large bomber pieces of gear for the anchor. I perched there in the bomb bay chute, the slab of granite sweeping briefly down at a steep angle before it ended in nothingness for 600 feet. Regaining my breath, I slowly hauled the rope in and loop each coil through a sling in the anchor to prevent its escape. It was with some satisfaction that I noted both Robin and Kashi needed rope tension to complete the pitch too.

Next, it was Robin's turn to get us higher. The easy crack I was anchored in steepened and narrowed to a nasty off-width above. Robin choose a variation to the left, involving intricate, sustained, and hard-to-protect face climbing. It was a great lead and now the two hardest pitches were behind us. But the climb was far from over. Easy cracks above fooled me and I climbed into a dead end. After down-climbing, I traversed right on a wonderful hand traverse to a prominent white scar in the rock.

Chapter 6

It led to a small ceiling and when I peeked over, there above me was an amazing 100-foot, near-vertical sea of knobs. I went from one to the next, clipping into the odd, welcome fixed piton or attaching runners around the various knobs with a slipknot. According to some authorities, this is the mental crux of the route, but here, I was flying.

The wall ended and I stepped onto a large, flat ledge. Here my rope ended too. I needed ten more feet but it was taut as piano wire. I tugged and tugged and gained only a few inches.

"ROBIN, I NEED MORE ROPE!"

I learned later he had untied from the anchor and climbed up ten feet. At the back of the ledge sat a pile of talus but also some good cracks for the anchor. Once on belay, I looked up, and seeing the rim close, knew with a rush of good feeling we had it in the bag. Kashi, who had never led a pitch before, took the lead for the last low-angle scramble to the top. It was 7 PM on a balmy and delightful Yosemite summer evening. Other parties were topping out on longer, harder routes and we congratulated each other. There had been a couple of parties below us earlier, but there was no sign of them now. We devoured the rest of our cheese and bagels feeling fine in the afterglow of our first El Cap climb. There was a feeling that more El Cap routes could be on the horizon. Suddenly the sun exited behind Middle Cathedral Rock and we had to scoot. None of us knew the East Ledges descent.

Scrambling down to the east we stopped at the first set of rappel bolts. Kashi dropped a coil in the rope and the ensuing tangle took a good ten minutes to unsnarl. Evening rapidly approached.

"What do you think? Should we bivouac here tonight?" I said.

No harm would come to us on such a warm night. But Robin wanted to push on. Darkness was upon us after the first rappel. I pulled out my headlamp, but the others were not so equipped.

One headlamp would have to suffice for three.

I had to search around for the next rappel station. When the others arrived, we pulled the ropes, but they hung up off to the side. No amount of pulling would budge them. For the second time, I wondered aloud if we should stop until morning when Robin noticed a series of ledges leading toward our stuck ropes. Cautiously I tiptoed along these holds for about 50 feet, risking a long pendulum swing. The headlamp illuminated the tiny holds and miraculously I was able to free the rope and get back without harm. The third rap delivered us to terra firma. Our troubles were still not over. The ropes stuck again, perhaps crossed near the anchor. It took the combined strength of three of us to retrieve the two 9mms. They were stretched so thin in the process that I decided then and there to retire my rope from any further duty.

The rope work was over but now we had a thousand feet of cross-country descent illuminated by one weak flashlight. No trail was evident, which should have been the case for this popular East Ledges descent. We had likely found an older rappel route fallen into disuse. The way led through thick forest, over downed trees, into dry cobbled creek beds. We had been on the go all day, but nobody was tired, only exhilarated. The others followed my weakening beam of light as best they could. About an hour later we connected with the main East Ledges trail. Then another hour of easier descent as the full moon rose above the valley walls.

Finally, at about 11 PM, we stood on the floor of Yosemite Valley. But Scott, who was supposed to meet us, was not there. The moonlit pavement was deserted of all cars. No matter. We were feeling a powerful, residual, positively euphoric energy. Striding along the highway, no more need for the headlamp, I felt that I could keep walking like this straight out of the park and all the way home to Napa. Surely at El Cap Meadow we would see Scott. But his van was nowhere to be seen. He was

Chapter 6

gone and with him were Robin and Kashi's sleeping bags and pads. We learned the next day when he reappeared that the rangers busted him for sleeping in the van and he left the park.

The night was cooling off a bit now and my friends were looking at an uncomfortable night without shelter. My own gear was in my truck. But wait, I remembered there were not one but two extra sleeping bags plus a pad and a blanket. My Boy Scout habit of carrying back-up gear was paying off. Thus, fully equipped, we sneaked off to our usual rogue campsite in the woods under El Cap, for a slumber worthy of our efforts. By daybreak, we were gone before the rangers could discover our lair.

Chapter 7
The Sur

The late Ed Ricketts, marine biologist and the 'Doc' of John Steinbeck's Cannery Row felt there was something strange and very sinister about the Coast and Lobos, in which he was not alone, as I heard the same tale from many other sources in one form or another. The essence of it was that people would suddenly feel overshadowed and be seized by a feeling of terror. Once when Ed Ricketts was climbing the mountains above Lobos in the Carmel Highlands with Rich and Tal Lovejoy (Rich was a reporter on the Monterey Herald), all three of them were suddenly overcome with terror. A nameless invisible menace seemed about to attack them. They ran all the way down the mountain to the highway where their car was parked, exchanging not a single word and sped to town.

Ed gave this phenomenon a name. He called it The Terror.
—From A Wild Coast and Lonely: Big Sur Pioneers *by Rosalind Sharp Wall*

I came across this astounding quote many years after my own experience of The Terror in 1997. My love affair with the Sur had begun decades before this when I spent a seminal week in the Big Sur backcountry on a Sierra Club Highlight trip in the spring of 1970. For the uninitiated, a Highlight trip is a luxury backcountry outing in which horses carry all the heavy gear to camp each day. Our only responsibility was a small daypack. Our itinerary took us into the heart of the Ventana Wilderness, from Bottcher's Gap past the famed Double Cone, and eventually over the Coast Ridge Road to Pfeiffer. I spent most of my time hiking in the company of three other young people and singing Neil Young songs around the campfire at night. But it was the old-timers who had the most impact on me. Some were upwards of 70 and 80 years old but still possessed encyclopedic memories for every tree and wildflower we came across, both common and scientific names. I learned about the Santa Lucia Fir, endemic to this area, poppies and lupine, the charming Baby Blue Eyes, False Solomon's Seal, and many others.

I returned to Big Sur each spring throughout the 1970s and beyond, either with friends or more commonly alone, to soak up the special magic this country breathes—a magic that can be found nowhere else in the world. Hitchhiking north from Santa Barbara was my common form of transportation then. I often carried a plant guidebook and would stop at each new flower to identify it. Once I borrowed Philip Munz's *Shore Wildflowers of California Oregon and Washington*, a little hardcover book that got water damage during one of the common spring rains. A librarian refused to take it back and made me buy the book for a whopping five dollars.

My first trip alone was unintentional—a friend didn't show up, so I hiked out of Posts (long before the hotel went in) on a loop trip to Sykes Hot Springs. These were formative years when I challenged myself to go to the most remote places I could find, often seeing nobody else for up to a week. Before it was so popular, I was a minimalist, carrying no tent, no stove, sometimes not even a flashlight for the dark nights. Eventually, I became familiar with every trailhead on the Coast save one.

In March of 1997, I was invited by my publisher Bob Lorentzen to hike a large portion of the Coast Ridge Road/Trail in Big Sur as part of his research for a new book called *Coastwalk*. With us would be his friend from Monterey, Garret. By this time, I thought I been through it all and seen it all. But on this trip, the Sur had a wildcard to play.

After meeting in Monterey, Bob, Garrett and I arrived at the

Chapter 7

Post Ranch Inn, now radically transformed since my first solo outing in 1972, when all that existed was a gate, a trail sign, and a herd of cows that seemed to bar my way. With heavy packs and a steep grade ahead of us, we felt like self-appointed beasts of burden. Cresting the Coast Ridge Road at Terrace Creek Junction, we spent the first night at Timber Top.

There, at the same campsite, I recalled another night from the Sierra Club outing decades before. The memory is a sweet one. The night was warm and humid. Far out in the Pacific, a ghostly, horizon-long fog bank waited patiently for currents of wind to usher it ashore. A slight drizzle fell intermittently, and we wondered if it would rain, but we were not worried, even though we had no tents set up. A young girl and I snuggled together in our shelter of sleeping bags, exchanging kisses, while a few raindrops gently caressed the sides of our faces.

Bob, Garret, and I were out early each morning and the days went by slowly and uneventfully, but also majestically—the juxtaposition of the ocean and mountains that entranced Robinson Jeffers equally entrancing us. We caught sight now and then, far to the east, of the Ventana Double Cone formation that has given the Ventana Wilderness its name. We also noticed, far below us in a meadow to the west, the fleeting image of a swiftly moving mountain lion. We came to Partington Ridge Trail junction, still the only trail on the Coast I haven't explored. Down this ridge, much closer to the ocean, is where the author and raconteur Henry Miller lived and wrote his way into the hearts of the locals. Near dark, we came to Cold Springs, a year-round water source, and made this our second camp. I felt tired and sore and went to bed early.

The next day, a few wispy clouds heralded a weather change as we passed Anderson Peak and walked through a gate that proclaimed "Marble Peak Ranch 1885". The cabin nearby looked unoccupied.

It was near here, in April 1974, that my girlfriend Mary and

I endured part of a ferocious three-day storm in a 3mm thin, double-walled, plastic tube tent. Now anachronistic, it was then a popular way to tent cheaply. Tube tents were simple to pitch — you make an A-frame with parachute cord tied between two trees and 'secure' it with clothespins. It was open to the elements on both sides. The lightning was striking only a quarter-mile away on Anderson Peak as all-night torrents of rain formed a pool of water at the foot of our miserable shelter.

In the morning Mary and I had a respite from the rain, but everything was a sodden mess and ten miles separated us from Highway 1. Soon after starting, we came across tire tracks in the muddy road and traced them back to a Quonset hut. Inside, the heat from a woodstove gave us a nearly suffocating welcome. We were in luck. One of the men who monitored this weather station was driving to town. The high clearance, four-wheel-drive truck was a good match for the conditions as we slopped two feet deep through mud holes and slid sideways around corners. The driver handled it brilliantly, but Mary later told me it was the second time in twelve hours that she thought her time on earth was up.

As Bob, Garret, and I walked the same ridge road, and as clouds once again gathered around Anderson Peak, I hoped that this present weather front was not a harbinger of similar things to come. All day the cloud cover slowly increased and by the time we reached the single table and stove that is Upper Bee Camp, the sky was uniform gray. Our dinner was a simple affair and we retired before dark on this somber evening. The next morning, yellow and orange light shone from beneath dark, heavy clouds, but we never saw the sun itself. The clouds covered the sunrise quickly and ominously as it grew steadily colder. On the trail that afternoon we took a wrong turn and lost our way. Back on track, we made camp early and long before nightfall I had pitched my tiny Eureka tent with the Hobbit-hole entrance that required shoehorning your way inside and tried

Chapter 7

to warm up. Rain fell heavily, then snow, then sleet. In the morning we found our tents covered in rime ice. Well below freezing inside and out, the water bottle I had accidentally left outside had frozen solid. All that day I struggled to stay warm. Our unmaintained trail became overgrown with chaparral and we fought our way through wet brush. I photographed a dead bird on the ground, perhaps killed by the extreme weather.

The skies started to clear towards day's end and Cone Peak came into view some miles away. This is the second-highest peak in the Sur at 5,155 feet, and the highest coastal peak in the United States. To hike from sea level to the summit requires more elevation gain than summiting Half Dome from Yosemite Valley. There is an old fire lookout on top, unmanned like so many these days.

We passed a dilapidated old sign that marked the junction to Cook Springs Camp—one distant spring I had spent a night there alone with the wind moaning through the treetops and struggling for hours to get rain-soaked wood to cook my meager dinner. We came to another junction where my companions dropped off the Coast Ridge Trail and headed down to Trail Springs Camp. I stayed on the ridgetop to rest and catch the last rays of weak sun. I lay down on a bed of pine needles, hoping to garner some warmth, but instead the sky began to spin above me. Overhead, I focused on a massive Ponderosa Pine, hoping to stop the spinning. An anxious and unwelcome thought intruded itself on my consciousness—this tree might fall and crush me. My rational mind knew this was foolishness. I had spent a thousand nights under trees safely. But the feeling was too strong to resist. The fear forced me up and away. Something was overcoming me.

I walked through a madrone forest, a gentle, slightly sloping path covered in slick pads of leaves. I was gripped with a new fear of sliding off the path and getting injured. I placed my feet carefully, each step slow and methodical as if this simple path was a steep ice slope and each step could be my last. Twenty-five years of backpacking and mountain climbing seemed to mean nothing now, and all those climbs on vertical rock walls in Yosemite were of no avail.

At camp, my heart sank further. Trail Springs Camp was dark, dank, and unappealing. Years before, not liking the vibe, I avoided spending even one night here and had continued on to Goat Camp, one of the loveliest sites in all of Big Sur. Bob and Garrett seemed unaware of my unstable mental state and I was afraid to tell them. There was only one tiny site left in this dismal camp, so small it wouldn't take a tent. I lay out my tarp, pad, and bag. Fortunately, there was to be no rain that night. A roaring fire moderated the plummeting night temperatures. Garrett handed me a hot mug of soup and I held it in both hands, shaking slightly and terrified I might drop it. I shivered and couldn't warm up, despite wearing all I'd brought and standing close to the fire. Bob and Garrett talked while I remained silent. Some intruder was wrapping its web-like tentacles around my brain.

I warmed up some in my sleeping bag but couldn't sleep, gripped by an inchoate terror. Bob and Garrett retired when the fire died down. A nighthawk made its spooky call. Images began to flash through my mind unbidden, images of madness, unspeakable acts of the night. I saw dark, hooded, Satanic figures with instruments of torture, and their victims caught in the horror. These acts of craziness and insanity seemed connected with the place I was now occupying. In other words, they seemed to have happened right here. I wrestled with these horrifying images and thoughts for hours. But some part of me could still witness what was going on, so I refrained from waking the others. Finally, far into the night, I fell asleep.

In the gray morning, I was marginally better but exhausted. The uphill trail to Cone Peak junction was strewn with fallen trees and it took great effort to hike around them. Garrett had reached the saddle but returned to carry my pack the last few hundred yards. I waited while my companions did a side hike to Cone Peak's summit. They hadn't asked questions and must have assumed I was simply tired. After an hour, I grew impatient and began constructing a message with small stones spelling out my decision to hike out. They returned just before I finished it, and in my embarrassment, scattered the stones before they could see them. We left the forest and walked into weak sunshine. The weather was unsettled and cold and I only removed my heavy down coat near the trailhead.

Once in the car, both my body and brain started to thaw out. It's as if whatever entity had gripped me couldn't get past those car doors. By the time we got to Monterey and Garrett's place, I was nearly normal. That night I spilled the story to Garrett's wife while she listened sympathetically and without undue alarm as if she'd heard similar stories before. At night I slept like a stone and in the morning, all traces of the experience had gone, my mind was clear.

This was a singular incident and nothing remotely like it has occurred before or since. I've often thought about this ordeal. The rational mind comes up with sensible explanations—maybe I exerted more calories than I ingested, the brain was low on blood sugar and hallucinations followed. Unique as this experience was, I've felt the mystical energy of Big Sur in other ways. I don't feel this kind of power anywhere else on earth. One thing is certain after fifty years of mountain travel—the two most bone-chilling storms I've ever been through have been in Big Sur and both were in the Marble Peak area. It wasn't the eight-day monsoon storm in the Sierra, or lightning and thunderstorms in British Columbia, or hailstones the size of baseballs in Colorado, nor even outings in the Dolomites of Italy or the Karakorum Himalaya. It has been my fate that such extremes have been reserved only for the domain of Big Sur.

Tales do abound, you hear them all the time. One story goes that a group of hikers lost the trail and crossed the entire

Ventana range from east to west without ever re-finding a trail—it took them 30 days to cross 25 miles as the crow flies. The story may be apocryphal but it's hardly the point. It *could* be possible. When you venture beyond Highway 1 and the Ventana's designated trails you encounter some of the most rugged country on Earth. As for disembodied entities, mystical experiences, or unseen spirits, take it as you will. I still don't know what to think, except that my respect for this strange and beautiful country remains as strong as ever.

> *I might not have quite believed Ed if I had not had an identical experience in the company of Frank and Marjory Lloyd of Carmel. (Both were editors of the Carmel Pine Cone). They came down to Mill Creek to visit the old deserted limekiln, three miles up the canyon, and we got there about noon. It was a hot day. We sat in the blazing sun, feeling relaxed and happy, looking at the old deserted houses with their broken-down stair cases and cracked windows gaping blank as broken teeth....Above us was the huge cracked limekiln oven. Bees were buzzing. The atmosphere seemed peaceful. We were hungry and about to open our paper bags to eat our picnic lunch when suddenly, all three of us, without saying a word to each other, rose and started back down the trail. We walked fast; we didn't run, but we felt like running. I, for one, was terrified. We did not speak until we had safely reached the road near the wooden county bridge where our car was parked three miles down canyon.... We did not know what had frightened us, only that we had been terrified. Something nameless had threatened us and we had fled.*
>
> *That is why I believed Ed Ricketts.*
>
> Rosalind Sharp Wall

Chapter 8
Tenaya: Yosemite's Lost Canyon

The demagogues ... who have already caused the death of several civilizations, harass men so that they will not reflect; manage to keep them herded together in crowds so that they cannot reconstruct their individuality in the one place where it can be reconstructed, which is in solitude.
   —Jose Ortega Y Gasset, Man and People

Steve Roper's glowing account of his solo, two-day descent of Tenaya, appearing in Summit magazine's Spring 1990 issue, was the original inspiration for our own adventure nine years later.

Very close to the heart of Yosemite Valley, between the popular tourist destinations of Tenaya Lake and Mirror Lake, lies the rugged and virtually unknown canyon of Tenaya. Of the four million people who visit Yosemite each year, perhaps only a dozen make this challenging and rewarding eight-mile journey. John Muir, the great conservationist and a leading mountaineer of his day, took the only serious fall of his life in the Inner Gorge of Tenaya. Slipping on glacially polished rock and taking a somersaulting fall, he was stopped a whisker away from an even greater, probably fatal, drop. Once he awoke from unconsciousness, he found he was completely unharmed. Muir, who had been a city captive for months before this, admonished himself—"There, that is what you get by intercourse with stupid town stairs and dead pavements." Later, he wrote—"Between Mt. Watkins and Cloud's Rest, the canyon is accessible only to mountaineers, and it is so dangerous that I hesitate to advise even good climbers, anxious to test their nerve and skill, to attempt to pass through it."

His words are just as true today. Those who would explore it must be confident in most aspects of mountaineering, have good route-finding skills, and be willing to wade or swim in the chill waters of Tenaya Creek. People are rescued in there every year, and so many have died or simply disappeared that park rangers call it the 'Bermuda Triangle of Yosemite'.

The watch alarm rang at 4 AM after a miserable night at Camp Curry. Two or three hours of sleep was my pittance due to noisy neighbors and the thin canvas walls of our tent. Mac, one of my two hiking partners this day, was refreshed and ready to roll. Little wonder—I've seen him fall asleep in a fully lit backcountry ski lodge during a raucous party. He used to drive his airplane-phobic wife crazy by falling asleep before takeoff.

Our shuttle driver appeared right at the appointed time—a sweet young girl from the Yosemite Association to drive us to Tenaya Lake and leave our car at Camp Curry on the return. Phil, who rounded out our hiking threesome, had arranged for this crucial service with some charm and a hefty but undisclosed sum of money. Park policy still forbids overnight parking on Tioga Road after mid-October, a rule I tested, and which cost me $250 the previous year. Halfway along the Tioga Road, the introductory chatter died down and suddenly we all sensed the girl's nervousness. Then it hit us—a young girl, three older men, a deserted wilderness road, and the murders of two women and two girls that were in the headlines! One of the victims was from the Yosemite Institute. Without alluding directly to the incidents, Mac was able to lighten things up by assuring her that he was an ordained priest in the Episcopal Church.

The temperature was a frigid 31° F at the empty trailhead at 6 AM. I still felt haggard from little sleep and a forced meal, but this was neither an auspicious nor uncommon start for such a big outing. Fortunately, we had prepared well for this late-

Chapter 8

October canyoneering adventure. We had not just one but three different photocopied descriptions, including one from RJ Secor's book, *The High Sierra*. We hoped to improve on his recommendation of a two-day trip by doing it in one long, dawn-to-dusk effort. Our rucksacks contained the essentials—calorie-busting lunches that could serve double duty as dinner in case we have to bivouac, water bottles with Gatorade, a water purifier, a 9mm perlon rope, climbing harnesses, rappel devices, and a first-aid kit.

We said goodbye to the young lady, then promptly got lost in the dark. Losing a half hour, we stumbled into the dry, sandy creek bed of Tenaya and were on our way. As the darkness waned and the headlamps were turned off, we came to Admonition Point, where a metal sign warned of danger ahead and to return to Tioga Road. Immediately beyond was Waterwheel Bowl, a square mile of delightful, low-angle granite slabs with a wisp of a trickling stream amid scattered patches of ice. During spring snowmelt, Tenaya Creek puts on a spectacular display of waterwheels like the more famous one in the Grand Canyon of the Tuolomne.

Waterwheel Bowl, Tenaya Canyon, late October

Gaining confidence now, we made good time through the flat, pine-forested, mile-long Glacial Valley. Fleetingly, and prematurely, I wondered if this outing was overrated. Our reverie ended suddenly at the lip of a massive drop off. Climbers aren't prone to vertigo, but this would have been a good location for it. We couldn't see it, but we knew from the map that the 600-foot Pywiack Falls, Yosemite's least-known major waterfall, was just over the edge. We crossed the creek above the falls and scrambled up a massive dome, commanding sublime views of Cloud's Rest, Half Dome, and Glacier Point Apron. Below us was a sobering sight—a glacially polished tongue of granite pitched at 35–40 degrees, plunging a thousand feet into Lost Valley. It was here that Muir, traveling in the opposite direction, stated, "I escaped from the gorge about noon, after accomplishing some of the most delicate feats of mountaineering I ever attempted."

Our rope would do no good here on this slab the equivalent of ten rope lengths, and so smooth that it afforded no suitable anchors. We'd have to follow in Muir's style as well as his footsteps. There were shallow cracks to use as hand and footholds, but mostly this was slab climbing, where a reliance and confidence in the friction between your shoes and the rock is paramount. Mac found his own way down while Phil and I looked for an alternate start. We ended up hanging from aspen branches in a spring-fed thicket, just above the seep water and icicle-laced granite slab. It took an hour of extremely delicate friction climbing before we arrived safely in Lost Valley. Meandering through house-sized boulders we reached the creek, silently wondering how much worse the infamous Inner Gorge could be.

The sun was about to peek over the rim thousands of feet above us. A distant tree was backlit in splendor. Floating so lightly, as if free of gravity, was a silvered web of filament, then a dozen, then hundreds of them. We didn't understand what they were at first and only wondered at the beauty and grace of

Chapter 8

the sight. Later I came across this passage from Muir:

> *The air on the divide is full of insects and when seen in the sunlight with the eyes protected by the crest of the mountain they appear like transparent flecks of silver. I have observed the air full of silvered cobwebs above the summit of (Mt.) Lyell. None of these insects or webs are at all visible under other circumstances.*

The newly arrived sunshine cheered us with warmth, searing the alder tree leaves a bright red. Moments after commenting on the unusual number of bear scat atop creek boulders, a great rustling occurred in the streamside vegetation. A medium-sized bear looked back briefly before doing a disappearing act. We got the feeling that this wild bear hadn't been hanging around valley dumpsters. As the boulder hopping ended, Tenaya Creek gathered force, the ground dropped away, and a waterfall sluiced wickedly down glassy walled sides into a shadowed cavern. We had arrived at the Final Jumping Off Place, the start of the Inner Gorge.

Here we stopped for lunch and pondered how to get past this obstacle. I tried to eat a sandwich, but it was like chewing cotton batting. Phil wasn't eating much either. Only Mac, the man of faith, seemed unaffected, chowing down on his roast beef and cheese. During the break, I explored the narrow, horizontal ramp at the base of a sheer cliff above and found a rare piece of history in this seldom-visited canyon. The initials SLF were carved into the rock face. They belonged to S.L. Foster who made annual excursions alone between 1909 and 1937 (except for the years 1917–18 and 1921) naming many of the topographic features. This section must have been daunting to Foster. He discovered a way out by following the high and exposed ledge, a hundred feet above the roaring chasm, which narrows at one point to only a foot wide.

No Mere Pastime

Returning to a lower ledge, we found the two-bolt rappel anchor and were soon safely downstream from the impassable waterfall. Once in the maw of the beast, it was not so difficult. Flat, rocky passages were interrupted by sheer drop-offs, one a huge boulder the size of a Beverly Hills mansion. To get around these obstacles required either down-climbing, rappelling, or a choice we could thankfully avoid on this chilly day—swimming. At one point huge boulders formed a narrow squeeze that S.L. Foster called the Keyhole. We pushed our packs through first, then squirmed through the barely body-width slot. The gorge narrowed further, becoming more and more beautiful, the sky above a mere slice of blue, the emerald-green water quietly gathering into yet another gem of a pool. Wedged in the press of the narrow canyon walls we were treading on sacred ground, privileged to pass where for most of the year the river tempest would mean instant oblivion. Finally, we came to the end of the gorge and, as the air temperature had risen some twenty degrees since dawn, we stripped off our clothes and took a ritual swim in the frigid water. The pool was a neon, emerald-green color, its inlet a concave tongue of smooth granite looking like burnished silver in the late afternoon autumn light.

Mac in the Keyhole, Tenaya Canyon

Chapter 8

The technical part of the day was over so we packed away our climbing gear. But looking west we were dismayed by how far we had to go. No time to slow down now. It was already past mid-afternoon with only two hours of daylight left. We plunged down a rocky slope that turned surprisingly wide and flat. To our right, the stunning and rarely seen Mt. Watkins reared a full 3,000-feet into the sky, a twin to the better known El Capitan. We alternated between streambed and adjacent forest, eventually choosing the forest when the terrain dropped steeply again. Our ancient hunter instincts revived as we connected one faint animal path after another. An occasional cairn was the only sign that others had passed this way. Lengthening shadows were quickly consuming the light and still we continued to drop and drop through endless pine and oak forests.

Quietly, without any warning, the remains of a flood-damaged bridge over Tenaya Creek appeared. Then, an actual trail—we were relieved to know that Mirror Lake was very close now. We gladly gave up decision-making and route finding and put our brains on autopilot. The tourists were long gone from Mirror Lake. We paused before entering the 'rural metropolis' of Yosemite Valley to enjoy a last moment of solitude. Alpenglow bathed the Northwest Face of Half Dome in golden light, but the canyon of Tenaya had been swallowed by black, brooding shadow. Our bodies were buzzing with nearly audible fatigue after twelve hours on the go. Our legs may have been leaden, but our hearts were light as those silvered cobwebs floating gracefully downwind in the final light of day.

A version of this chapter first appeared in the Sept/Oct 2000 issue of *California Explorer*.

Chapter 9
El Capitan: Viva Los Chicos Viajos

The worst days of our lives and the best days merged and became indistinguishable. Suffering, remembering, laughing, and climbing again turned out to be inseparable elements of the same life- a life in contrast to an existence comfortable and predictable but without the light and darkness that brings us alive.
—Joe Kelsey

Four hundred and fifty vertical feet above the base of El Capitan, it was early evening on the first day of a three-day climb in June 2000 and my mechanical rope ascenders were failing. When working properly, Jumars should slide upwards along the rope easily but hold any downward weight securely. Alarmingly, the right Jumar was slipping several inches before holding. My only other security was a figure-eight back-up knot I tied to my harness every 25 feet or so. If the Jumar failed, I was looking at a long fall. For me, the climb could already be over.

"Mac! Can you get me a pair of ascenders at the Mountain Shop?" I asked one of my two partners on the ground.

"I'm on my way, Bud!"

Our walkie-talkies were proving useful already.

The day had started slowly, stuck behind three parties on this world-famous route first done in 1958. The Nose, as Warren Harding called it, is still the most popular route on El Cap, despite the addition of nearly 100 new routes. The first ascent party had doggedly taken 45 days over a year and a half, slowed by park regulations and logistical difficulties never before encountered. Our plan of three days was about average for a modern party. By contrast, Alex Honnold and Tommy Caldwell had raced up The Nose in 2018 in under two hours.

Four pitches up was Sickle Ledge, a painful reminder of my former high point eight years ago, accompanied then, as now, by my friend and guide, Armin Fisher. The intimidation factor had been too much for me and we'd bailed in favor of Washington Column. The South Face of the Column had been my first big wall success.

The traffic jam above prompted me to return to the ground to prepare the haul bags with food, water, and gear. Much later, lulled by a gentle wind, I was startled out of a nap by Mac's voice on the walkie talkie.

"Kenny, Armin wants you to get the haul bags to the base. We're on our way down."

"But they weigh a hundred and fifty pounds!"

"Armin says just do what you can, Kenny."

I groaned. Our 33 quarts of water weighed over 65 pounds alone. Luckily Sean, a photographer from the Napa Valley Register here to document our climb, volunteered to carry the smaller haul bag. The main bag I carried was over a hundred pounds and, as I discovered too late, lacking a functional hip belt. The base was only a quarter-mile away, but I had to stop and prop the 'pig' on logs and rocks a dozen times en route. I was no spring chicken, and neither was Mac, both of us perilously close to the half-century mark. Fortunately, Armin, our rope gun, was still in his prime.

Up above, Armin had solved the traffic jam dilemma with patience and tact. The other parties eventually realized they would be better off letting him pass. Armin trailed their lead ropes when they tired, and quickly climbed two pitches past Sickle Ledge, fixed ropes, and returned to the ground. But the day was far from over. Armin immediately started preparing to return to Sickle with the main haul bag, allowing us to move quickly the next day. This change in plans transpired with an

Chapter 9

agreement that our party would go first on the fixed ropes, starting at 4:30 the next morning, giving the slower parties time to reach the first good bivouac ledge, Dolt Tower, a thousand feet up.

When Armin and I returned from our task, it was nearly dark. Mac met us at the truck with cold beers and a brand-new pair of Petzl rope ascenders, a bargain at $109. The climb was back on again for me.

At 1 AM, everyone was asleep but me, my monkey mind chattering incessantly. A late dinner or the overly warm night didn't pass muster as an excuse. It was a classic case of big-wall jitters. For the second time in eight years, I was thinking about a bailout from the Nose. When Armin's watch alarm beeped at 4 AM, I confided a bad case of nerves.

"Don't worry man, you'll be a wall rat by day's end."

Even though I've been up two Grade Vs, Washington Column and the Leaning Tower, the Nose would be my first Grade VI, three times the height of any previous outings. Mac and I had been training for a year, working the gym weights three times a week and climbing every weekend. On each outing, our target was to climb a thousand feet a day. I couldn't have been in better physical condition. But damned if I didn't have to slay my inner saboteur one more time.

We choked a bagel and cheese down our throats with a chaser of spring water. At 4:30 AM the night was already losing its grip and we needed to motor. I clamped the new Petzls on a brand-new Edelweiss 60-meter rope, made sure the daisy chain was the right length to allow rests between upward progress, and fitted my boots into the five-step aiders. The new ascenders bit perfectly and I never worried about them again. Once past the initial rope slack, the ascension process was simple, like dance steps—raise left leg and arm together, raise right leg and arm together, repeat for 3,000 feet…

By mid-afternoon, my fatigue from the sleepless night was

replaced by euphoria at my surroundings. We pulled onto El Cap Tower, a thousand feet from the base at 6 PM. One of El Cap's best crash pads, it was perfectly level, four feet wide, and long enough for the three of us to stretch out fully. Armin and Mac fixed two pitches above while I readied the site for the night. Our day had gone smoothly, warm in this first week of June but not hot, and the afternoon winds that can flay you were like gentle caresses. Even a snagged rope around a flake above Dolt Tower had come loose with two deft twists, avoiding a time-costly rappel.

Partners Mac and Armin on El Cap Tower, the Nose, El Capitan

Chapter 9

When my partners returned, we propped our sleep pads against the wall and let our bare feet dangle over the drop. We were home. There was a brief scare when the can opener couldn't be found and then we pounced on dinner — cold Dinty Moore beef stew and beans straight from the can, bagels and cheese, and — best of all — Del Monte fruit cocktail. To our left, a party of three, hanging one above the other like beads on a string, were still not ready for the night. Across the valley, Middle Cathedral Rock's massive gray bulk formed a backdrop for the green gem of El Cap Meadows. The Merced River meandered through it in lazy loops.

Before total darkness, a British party hauled onto Dolt Tower, two pitches below. I checked my daisy chain attached to the main anchor, slipped into my bag, and passed out without awakening until dawn.

On big walls — if your intestinal timing is good — you head to the poop deck first thing. By mutual consent and common sense, it's as far from sleeping quarters as possible, however, if you're unlucky then it's located by smell alone. Present park regulations require climbers to carry human waste out and dispose of it properly, and almost everyone does now. We carried wagbags for that purpose. Your aim must be reasonably good, and the built-in double seal does the rest. It goes to the bottom of the haul bag every morning.

Our first objective, Texas Flake, resembles its namesake when seen from the ground. At the top, it's a cushy 6 inches wide but separated from the main wall by a 3-foot gap. To bridge this gap, you make a controlled fall, arms outstretched, looking into the 70-foot abyss below. From here the route would lead us to Boot Flake and the famous King Swing. For dozens of binoculared tourists at El Cap Meadow, this was the pitch to watch.

From the top of Boot Flake, Mac lowered Armin 70 feet down on the lead line. He began several short, horizontal back-and-forth runs until at a signal made a bid for a hold 30 feet to his left. He nailed it first try then clipped a bolt and repeated the procedure, securing a crack another 30 feet to the left. Armin's grace belied the difficulty—many climbers have exhausted themselves here (coming up short of the key holds can mean an out-of-control pendulum fall). Higher up, Armin found the belay and we lowered the haul bags out slowly on an old 30-meter line. Then Mac lowered me until I could climb up to the belay. Mac had to perform a horizontal rappel technique he'd learned only the previous day.

Mac seemed an unlikely candidate for an Episcopal priest until you got to know him. Funny, energetic, down to earth, and open-minded, he was the first one to show you his faults and his passions (my own faith lies outside the church, so I appreciate his lack of evangelicalism). Underneath was a deep and abiding faith in God and an exceptional gift to share it. Many are the conversations we've had about the nature of the universe. Mac's first climbing partner was Mugs Stump when they were both ski bums in Utah in the '70s. But while Mugs went on to a stellar career in alpinism, Mac's trajectory took him into the realm of the spirit. Mac and I met through one of his parishioners at the time he wanted to restart his climbing career. We became climbing partners thereafter, lasting for nearly a decade. I believe Mac's cheerfulness and confidence up there on El Cap had a lot to do with his faith. I couldn't have had two better partners than Mac and Armin.

The Great Roof loomed just above us. It was easily the most identifiable feature from the ground, and so large, with about 25 feet of overhang, so that a climber underneath would be in shadow all day. Our route beelined to the Roof, then traversed 50 feet to a tiny, marvelously exposed stance. When Armin finished the pitch, Mac lowered me out until I was directly under the belay. Without this precaution, I'd have had a wild and potentially dangerous swing. I released the lower-out rope and hung suspended from the single, 11mm line, now 2,000 feet

Chapter 9

above the valley, and twenty feet from the wall itself. My job was to follow the haul bags and free them if they hung up on an overhang or to push them off lower-angle slabs. This work was not easy, but it paled in comparison to Armin's efforts, doing all the leading and hauling.

Earlier, Mac and I found out what it was like to haul the pigs for part of a pitch. Our first efforts didn't move them an inch. Eventually, we succeeded, but it gave us increased admiration for our guide. To my left, Mac worked cleaning gear under the Great Roof. At the last awkward move, I threw a hand over to assist him. We stood on the inches-wide ledge as afternoon shadows lengthened, letting the great curving sweep of the Roof lead our eyes back to the valley floor. We just didn't know how it could get any better. Suddenly Phil, who'd just arrived in the Valley, was on the walkie talkie at El Cap Meadow, ecstatic to talk to us.

"I'm looking at you guys through binoculars and you're still tiny as insects!"

Two long pitches followed and near dark we crawled onto the ledge known as Camp 5.

"Is this it?" My disappointment was sharp.

Camp 5 slopes not only down but sideways too and is barely large enough to sleep two people. This place had been the scene of many fearful struggles in bad weather. One event involved 12 climbers and their gear all crammed together, while rainwater cascaded in waterfalls directly on the hapless victims. A few people have died there. Our stay, with balmy weather and no one else around, would be like taking tea on the veranda by comparison. Below us, there was no sign of the Brits who must have aborted their climb.

There was just enough time to eat and make camp before total darkness. Armin graciously left the ledge to us, jumaring a quarter rope length up to a higher ledge (half of his body length I noted in the morning). The down-sloping angles of Camp 5 are so intimidating that I clipped into several anchors and made sure the rope to my harness was taut, allowing zero movement toward the edge. In the night calm, we heard something metallic skitter away, pick up speed, and disappear into the void. We never discovered what it was. I expected a bad night, but exhaustion worked like a sleeping pill and soon I was fast asleep. Eight hours later I awoke in the same position I'd started in.

In the morning, two pitches delivered us to the spacious ledge called Camp 6. We scuttled our plans to hang out and enjoy the ambiance of this spectacular location and pushed on for the rim, only five rope lengths away.

The wall was beyond vertical now, about 95 degrees, but it made for smooth hauling of the pigs and I had more time to admire my surroundings. Flowers in bloom were growing out of the solid rock, looking like well-tended windowsill gardens. I came across resident frogs living their lives out where shadowed cracks and moisture provided a suitable environment. The swifts dive-bombed us at a hundred miles per hour. One stopped to check me out, hovering a foot from my face like a hummingbird. At the next belay, there was no ledge and we and our bags were suspended directly from anchor bolts. Mac camped out on top of the main pig and I slipped into my old nylon butt bag and hung like a spider from its threads. From our vantage, El Cap swept to the ground in a gigantic 'C', all 2,500 feet of it. We dubbed this place the Mother of All Hanging Belays.

Many climbers have felt the mystery of the upper thousand feet of The Nose, a true natural cathedral. Climbing these soaring dihedrals of cleaved rock were likened by Steve Roper to "living inside a cut diamond." The rock was ultra-smooth and massive up there, the light glancing off the polished rock can almost be too bright to bear, even with sunglasses. We felt the power of the place too. Every so often Mac and I exchanged looks of mutual disbelief and awe at our surroundings.

Our three ropes lay at my feet in controlled disorder.

Chapter 9

Suddenly the wind picked one end up and it went flying off the ledge. The winds up there were so strong that instead of falling down, the rope spilled out in a wavy horizontal line, all 180 feet of it. What a sight it was—the line dancing in the wind like a sentient creature. By some unseen eddy of air, the far end of the line suddenly swept around a buttress of rock and disappeared from view. I can't say why, but the beauty of that movement caught in my throat and I looked on entranced.

"Slack!" yelled Armin.

"Sorry!" I'd been holding the lead line tight and not paying attention.

By early afternoon, we were at the last stance below the colossal summit overhangs. In November of 1984, a Japanese team was caught in a storm right here. I'd been in the Tuolomne high country that same weekend, hiking in full winter clothing. Before leaving the park that trip, we got out at El Cap Meadow to give our respects to the Big Stone, not knowing until later the fate of the Japanese team, high above us, who froze to death.

Now I had an irritating tangle of rope to deal with while Armin was surging up the final pitch faster than I could feed it out. The legendary story of Harding's all-night bolting epic on this pitch is well known. He'd placed 1/4-inch bolts every six feet on this 120-degree overhanging final pitch. The old ones have since been replaced by safer 3/8-inch bolts, and Armin was soon on top without incident. I spent a good five to ten minutes making sure my setup was perfect. It had to be. After unclipping from this final anchor, I took the most terrifying swing of my life. When I came to rest in a gentle spin, I was a good 40 to 50 feet out from the wall due to the massive overhangs above. I waited until the spinning stopped then with infinite care removed a camera from my shirt pocket. I took a picture of my feet in aid stirrups, framing El Cap Meadow and the Merced River 3,000 feet below.

Jumaring final overhangs, 3,000 feet above Yosemite Valley

Only a hundred feet were left, and knowing it would soon be over, I tried to wring every last ounce of enjoyment from the moment. The high country of Tuolomne was now visible, the Clark Range and even Mts. Ritter and Banner, all in a fine mantle of snow. To the south lay Horse Ridge, underneath which lay the Ostrander Hut, a fine cross-country ski winter destination. The hazy, golden sun streaming in from the west was still warm. The haul bags were stuck on small ledges just above the great brow of El Cap and I freed them one last time. Then we finished the climb together.

Armin's belay was from a spacious ledge where we spent the night. It was a wild and windswept place up there on the summit, with venerable Western juniper trees scattered about that can grow for hundreds of years. Several liters of water were still in the haul bag so we left them for other parties who might top out thirsty. Phil, hiking in from the Tuolomne Road, arrived with a huge pack loaded with, of all things, cantaloupe and watermelon! Nothing could have been more welcome or celebratory. At the top of the Great Roof pitch the day before, Mac and I had

Chapter 9

remarked that we didn't know how it could get any better. Now we did. And to think I had almost bailed on this climb three days prior. Sometimes it's not easy distinguishing between one's intuition and just plain fear. This was not just my greatest climb, it was also one of the best experiences of my life. And I have my friends to thank for that.

Chapter 10
The Dolomites

Without mountains, we might find ourselves relieved that we can avoid the pain of the ascent, but we will forever miss the thrill of the summit, and in such a terribly scandalous trade-off, it is the absence of pain that becomes the thief of life.
—Craig D. Lounsbrough

Only a month after climbing El Capitan I was off to Italy for a week's climbing vacation by way of France. International flights like this one from San Francisco to Paris usually left me a wreck. There's something about the forced inactivity, the confinement, and lack of sleep that reminds me too much of Solzhenitsyn and *The Gulag Archipelago*. But I did all right until boarding the transport bus from Charles de Gaulle Airport to downtown. There was only enough room to stand and the driver, a bald man with bulging veins, looked maniacal. It was cold out and raining on the slick highway when suddenly the driver hit the brakes hard. My head slammed into a metal post while my luggage slid out of grasp. Goddamnit, I muttered. I look around but my fellow passengers were stone-faced. This wouldn't be the last time I had trouble with public transport in France.

Susan, who had been there a few weeks already, greeted me at the station downtown. Unlike me, my wife has a great talent for foreign language and was studying French at the Sorbonne through a special program sponsored by Napa Valley College. She adored the city. Though they put her up at a dorm, she stayed with me in a hotel while I was there for a week.

She had the subway system wired. We whipped around Paris while she chattered on. Normally shy and quiet, Susan blossomed here. She was like another person and that night in bed it felt like I was taking a lover instead of my wife of many years.

The blocks and blocks of somber, multi-story brownstone buildings looked dreary in the rain. But the outdoor markets were colorful and the many wonderful bookstores with books in many languages was a surprise. I had lots of time alone while Susan took classes during the day. When she was free we saw the usual sites like the Eiffel Tower and Arc de Triomphe, but my favorite places in Paris were the parks. I adore Parisian parks. I spent all day at the Jardin des Plantes, a botanical garden created in 1626 when Paris was the scientific center of the world.

The sun was breaking through the gloom the morning I stepped into the Jardin des Tuileries, where the King's Swiss guards were chased through the garden and massacred during the French Revolution. This day all was peaceful. I strolled enchanted while musicians played under a gazebo. There were fountains and ponds, flower gardens, tree-lined promenades, and lots of benches to rest on. Some accommodated families with picnic baskets, old folks with canes, and sunbathers enjoying the warmth after the rain. Some of these loungers were women who had nonchalantly tossed aside their blouses to sunbathe in their underwear.

I did not find Paris restaurants up to their vaunted reputation. Per capita, Napa Valley may have better, but I'll admit a possibility of bias. Happily, though, I found Parisians friendlier than reputed. For several mornings I breakfasted on poached egg and toast at a little outdoor café across from a small park where the gracious hostess made me feel right at home.

Paris though was not my main destination in Europe. I was more excited about the following week when I'd be in the Dolomites in the northeastern corner of Italy. Armin and I had our sights set on thousand-foot limestone cliffs where in the

Chapter 10

1930s legendary climbers like Emilio Comici were doing previously unimaginable climbs with grace and style. Since my early twenties, I'd read about climbing giants like Ricardo Cassin, Lionel Terray, and Walter Bonatti. Now, I'd be literally following in their footsteps.

At the travel agency, I was reassured when the agent spoke English well. She booked my train from Paris through Lyon in the south of France and across the border to Milan.

"Have you been to the train terminal before?" she asked.

"Oh no, I've never been to Paris before."

"It's a big place with six main terminals. You want the one called Gare du Lyon. Here's your ticket and directions, you won't have any trouble."

The subway I needed to take in the morning was only a half block from my *pension* but still, I walked it carefully to make sure there wouldn't be any problems. Susan and I said our goodbyes knowing that we would see each other next on another continent.

At 4 AM my watch alarm went off and I stumbled sleepily out the *pension* front door. All was very quiet for a big city. I took the short walk to the subway entrance as rehearsed and… .PHUCK! It had gone. How was this possible? The fucking entrance had disappeared. Was I in some parallel universe? Totally flustered now, I rushed back to the *pension* to talk to the late-night clerk.

"What happened to the subway entrance out here?"

Sleepily, she stared for a minute, perhaps thinking, Mon Dieu, *another* clueless American.

"That one closes up at night. You have to go one street over."

"Merci beaucoup," I said and rushed out into the dawn, my adrenaline overload about to fell me in the street. Subway entrances that close at night? Even Susan hadn't known that detail. Nothing else would go wrong, I promised myself.

But the train was late, and I was not the only one waiting

impatiently. At the Gare du Lyon terminal there were only a few minutes to spare.

I presented my ticket at the kiosk.

"Where are you going?" asked the man.

"Milan, it's right there on the ticket."

"No monsieur there is a mistake. This only goes to Lyon. For Milan, you must pay another 170 francs."

Christ! I could not imagine how the travel agent got this wrong. For a moment in my paranoid state I even wondered if she did this on purpose. Running with a heavy pack at top speed, I flew up the train steps as the door closed behind me.

When the adrenaline wore off, I noticed a sleeping man taking up two or three seats on the bench across the aisle. All other seating was full. He remained there until we crossed the border to Italy, at which time he left abruptly. Soon we'd be in Milan but, now I had an opportunity for some much needed rest, so took it and stretched out. Not five minutes later a uniformed employee marched by, tapped my shoes, which I had politely left off the seat, and commanded, "NO SLEEPING!"

Armin was there to meet me in Milan. It was good to see him. He grabbed my bags, tossed them in the back of his red Opel Kadett station wagon and we headed immediately for the mountains. Soon though we hit stop-and-go traffic in smoggy Milan. It felt like hometown Los Angeles except for the smaller vehicles and truck drivers cursing in Italian. With great relief, we turned off the highway for Lago di Garda, the largest lake in Italy. It was near sunset by the time we passed the upper lake and the last foothill vineyard. Armin thought this would make a good camp. A gorgeous orange sun was sinking. All was peaceful until a tractor with spray rig entered a row of grapes below us. The high-pitched whine of the PTO signaled a night operation of spraying fungicides for mildew prevention.

"Armin, do you think we can head up the road to a quieter location?"

Chapter 10

I found that there wasn't nearly as much space for freelance camping in Europe as America, but at twilight we finally located a quiet turnout where we'd be undisturbed. The last sound of the night was the spooky echo-like call of a Whip-poor-will, and his silhouetted form as he flew overhead was a shade blacker than the darkening sky.

I was so excited about climbing in the Dolomites. Though those walls can overhang for a thousand feet or more, free climbing is possible even on faces of over 100 degrees due to the profusion of various footholds and handholds on the highly featured limestone. It meant one could find hold combinations virtually anywhere. What I was not prepared for were the long, sometimes multi-pitch traverses that the old-school climbers used to bypass the harder sections on these fiercely intimidating climbs. Armin and I were on a route called the Michaeluzzi in the Sella Towers near the town of Cortina d'Ampezzo. We moved past an amicable party of Brits taking a smoking break on one of these 300-foot traverses.

Horizontal movement along a ledge or series of holds can be serious for the follower if they are not aware of possible pendulum falls. When the climb is more or less vertical, a fall for the second person is typically a matter of inches. But traverse falls can be dozens of feet and can lead to injury or death if you slam into an obstacle at high speed. I learned this lesson well when I was 23, in the Sespe Gorge above Ojai, California, when I took a thirty-foot pendulum, hitting my head twice before coming to rest. I was lucky to get away with a small concussion and some bloody scrapes. Ever since I've been especially attentive on traverses. Fortunately, Armin was placing gear or clipping old bolts and pitons which lessened the chance of 'swingtime'.

It was a warm afternoon in July and we were in shirtsleeves. A few hundred feet below at the base of the wall, two ibex butted heads in a jousting contest. Our route continued upward for the remainder of the climb. It was moderate in difficulty and the two of us were moving quickly. Even though our start time was early afternoon, we completed 12 pitches (over a thousand feet of climbing) by 5 PM and topped out with plenty of time to spare. The hike off the top was steep and exposed, so much so that metal cables had been installed for the safety of hikers and climbers alike. The day had been a great introduction to the Dolomites.

Here in the Dolomites, it was easier to find a free campsite than we'd experienced en route. We cooked up a simple but satisfying meal of fresh local produce, pasta and veggies with some local wine. Life doesn't get any better than this. Robert Redford once said he'd rather wake up in the middle of nowhere than any city on earth. I couldn't agree more. The night was clear and in the morning we woke to find frost on our sleeping bags.

An early drive took us over several passes to a Refugio where we took time out for continental breakfast and coffee. Outside the window of our breakfast nook, it was another perfect day in paradise. A half-hour hike took us to the base of the Pilastro est on the Tofana di Rozes. Our chosen route was first done in 1944 by Italian climbers Ettore Constantino and Romano Appolonio. According to our guidebook:

> *This is surely the most famous and popular route on this wall, thanks to its intrinsic beauty and perfect line. It is long and demanding... for local climbers, the classic of classics. In a postscript: "An Ettore Constantini masterpiece. Good shape required.*

The route starts out hard and just gets harder. There was no warm-up on this one. Classic Dolomite thin traversing low on the route gives way after a few hundred feet to several cruxes in the middle of the wall. If a party is not up to the grade, this is the place to turn around before getting committed. Above, we had to surmount two, 90-degree horizontal roofs. I struggled

Chapter 10

desperately on the second one, using only a two-step aider made out of a spare sling. Arms and legs trembled with fatigue I surmounted the roof and collapsed on a generous ledge. Breathing heavily, I struggled to regain composure, feeling completely spent, yet we were only halfway up. I despaired of my ability to continue. Continental breakfasts have never provided enough calories for me and I had nothing left. Armin dug out a Swiss chocolate bar and said, "EAT." He refused any of it and I devoured the whole thing.

Now I had the energy to look up, but I almost wished I hadn't. A jagged-edged, saw-toothed ridge of rock, separated widely from the main wall, rose skyward in an arc for 50 feet like the backbone of a dinosaur. The main wall was dark and looked smooth and water polished.

"How is that even considered climbable," I wondered aloud.

"You'll see," grinned Armin. "Hey, we're lucky today, this section is usually dripping with water!"

I watched in awe as Armin ascended one of the most famous passages in the Dolomites, the Schiena di Mulo, or Backbone of the Donkey. He was leading this unprotected, risking a long fall back to the ledge I stood on. About forty feet up he found a home-made wooden dowel with a hole into which he clipped a carabiner.

"This thing has got to be 60 years old," exclaimed Armin with glee.

"You're going to trust it?"

"Hell yeah, it's all there is."

Armin moved on after clipping the artifact and the difficulty eased. Soon, it was my turn. To be truthful I can't remember how I did it. The chocolate bar was having a good effect though. Maybe Armin by his passage had created some sort of temporary vortex where the gravitational effects were nullified. I got to the wooden peg and marveled at its solidity after two generations of exposure to wet conditions and sixty freezing

Alpine winters.

The fierce angle eased and I started to believe again I could make it. Armin's pace, if anything, increased. We topped out at 3 PM, only six hours after starting. We had just done 1800 feet of climbing (a Grade V in the parlance), averaging 300 vertical feet an hour. It was the longest one-day climb (for that grade) of my life and I felt fantastic. There must be something special in Swiss chocolate that American bars can't touch. An hour and a half later, after a rapid descent, we were being charmed by shop girls speaking German in a small mountain village close to the Austrian border. Armin knew some fellow guides here and they talked in German and Italian. I was told the guides were impressed that as a first-timer to the region, I was able to finish a Grade V in such good time. The other half of the story was Armin had a special talent he brought to each outing—a blend of optimism, confidence, encouragement, and irrepressible energy. All of his clients climbed beyond what they believed possible. One is simply swept upward like a hawk in a thermal. I was riding that high still, swimming in a sea of endorphins until the restaurant opened at 6 PM. The magic powers of Swiss chocolate held me until then.

That night was colder. We set up a tent a short way from the Opel Kadett (the Space Cadet, an old friend of mine used to call his). We slept as soundly as the surrounding limestone but were rudely awoken in the morning by a rough command in Italian. Armin flung the tent door open to find a uniformed Carabinieri in a poor mood explaining that we were illegally camped. Armin spoke fluent Italian but pretended to be a dumb American.

"Eh? no comprende."

"Leave now, you have five minutes!"

In five minutes flat we had packed our tent and personal gear and left, giddy with the relief of avoiding a fine.

On our third day in the Dolomites, we rested for the morning. I was reading John Muir's *Boyhood and Youth,* one of the most

Chapter 10

delightful memoirs ever. Muir grew up in Dunbar, Scotland, the family quarters on the second floor of what later became the Lorne Temperance Hotel. John and his brother Davy shared a bedroom whose dormer window looked out over the street. As boys typically do, John would challenge his younger brother to engage in adventures known in Scotland as 'scooters'.

Young John would climb out the window onto the sill using small hand- and footholds next to the dormer, then ascend the slick slate tiles to the pitched rooftop. He sat astride the high-pitched roof three stories above the street with the wind blowing a gale and threatening to blow him off. He then slipped down the tiles, managing to catch the sill before the vertical drop-off and get safely back inside. When Davy tried to emulate his brother, he froze with fear halfway up and John had to talk him down, grabbing his ankles as Davy slipped by and dragging him back into the bedroom. When Muir revisited his home fifty years later, he was amazed that with all his mountaineering experience, he found the feat was now beyond his abilities.

The Space Cadet made its way southeast of Cortina to a popular climbing area called Cinque Torre (Five Towers). These are small cliffs where amateurs and experts alike warm up for the bigger climbs. There must have been a hundred people there that day. We only climbed a few pitches, conserving our strength for the next day. A small market sold us some fresh tomatoes and mozzarella cheese kept fresh in a container of water. Our dinner that night was very simple, yet one of the most delicious of my life. I've never tasted that kind of quality at home.

Cima Piccola, Tre Cima di Lavaredo, Dolomites, Italy

The Spigalo Giallo (Yellow Edge) was first climbed by the legendary Emilio Comici, known as the 'Angel of the Dolomites', in a single day in 1933. One of his partners for this climb was Mary Varale, a pioneering alpinist who often climbed alone or with other women. The route is famous throughout the climbing world and often crowded. On the hike in, we stopped at a Refugio for tea and breakfast.

The weather was changing. Our warm and flawless days were giving way to clouds piling up on the horizon. We quick-footed it along the stony tread to the base of the Cima Piccolo di Lavaredo, standing in company with other larger giants like the Cima Grande. The Yellow Edge is a compelling thousand-foot fin of limestone that beckoned us to explore it. The rock quality is not the best but it's the *location* that makes this route a classic.

Chapter 10

The whole wall sweeps from the base into a huge concavity in the middle then crests at the top, giving one the feeling of 'surfing' a thousand-foot wave.

Today, we were once again in luck. A party of French climbers had decided to bail, finding the hauling of their pack too cumbersome. Armin and I were traveling lightly (all I had was a daypack) and we now had the route to ourselves. The first pitch was steep, polished, sweaty rock that led to a hanging belay. An amazing overhang led to a traverse on the second pitch. Then the angle eased as we moved into the middle section. Here, the rocks were big and blocky, and we made quick time. Soon, the wall reared up again regaining its stature. As I belayed, clouds were playing hide and seek with the hut below. The fog rose higher and higher and threatened to engulf me. I felt cut off from the world in an eerie state of limbo. The wind was rising too. I wore Armin's extra Thinsulite jacket, super light yet warm, worth its weight in gold up here.

From vertical, the wall continues to rear back until it overhangs ten or twenty degrees. A sixty-meter traverse on the 'brow' of the wall is one of the cruxes. Armin disappeared around a corner and I didn't hear from him for a while. The exposure was fabulous in that moment, the fog had dissipated, and the hut below was a tiny dark spot.

Then it was my turn. No wonder he took a while—the traverse was delicate, slightly rising, ever steepening. Simultaneously, the brow of the overhang tried to push me off, while below it was undercut and footholds were out of sight. Indeed, for one section there were only holds for hands and arms, legs free. Every once in a while I came to an ancient piton and unclipped the carabiner attached to it. Just when I thought the traverse would never end, there was Armin's face peeking over the edge. Our final pitch was technical and steep, near 5.10 in difficulty, a grade not achieved in the United States until decades later. Then it was over. On top, we had little time to celebrate as the wind suddenly picked up fiercely. We descended in a series of rappels to the long but easy talus slope and returned to the trail. Clouds were moving over the tops of the Tre Cima di Lavaredo and it would spell the end of our time in the Dolomites.

Armin on the traverse, Yellow Wall (Spigalo Giallo), Dolomites

That afternoon Armin was on the phone to friends and colleagues, but we were out of weather-luck. It was snowing in the Alps and our big finale on the Matterhorn or perhaps something on Mont Blanc had been dashed.

"September," said Armin, "that's the most settled weather in the Alps. Come back then," forgetting that every September was the single, busiest month of the year for me, locked into service

Chapter 10

with the grape harvest.

Our choice of campsite that night was a bit odd. An old churchyard with scattered graves and the lights and noise of the nearby town was a bit macabre even for Armin. We gave up after half an hour and drove far up the mountain, where swirling cold mists were preferable to the sweltering humidity of the lowlands. Our tent, set up in a crook of the winding road, seemed exposed to potential traffic but no cars come by that night.

Resigned to skipping our finale in the Alps, we descended to near-tropical weather on the coast and spent the last two days in shorts and t-shirts. We climbed at Monte Cucco where I got spanked. I was baffled by this kind of limestone with its tiny, widely spaced holds and no obvious rests. It felt like the trip's end. But before leaving we indulged ourselves by visiting Finale Ligure on the Bay of Genoa. Here on the Riviera, land of roses and carnations, the coast is dotted with picturesque seaside towns and their multi-colored houses draping the hillsides. Plenty of tourists lounge on the famous beaches, where toplessness is non-gender-specific.

All the way home the Space Cadet made ominous sounds like there was a badger in the tank instead of a tiger. We slowed to half-speed but managed to limp home. Armin's place in Alagna, underneath the great peak Monte Rosa, was made of stout timbers and slate roof tiles made to stand for centuries. Its look was softened by flower baskets on every window. Maria, his new wife, was working in Milan but I met his year-and-a-half-old daughter Isabella, a real charmer. She had a wide-open face with large, curious eyes and talked a blue streak.

My last evening in Italy was warm and balmy. A little village down the road was famed for its Italian ice cream. There wasn't a person there without a gelato cone in his or her hand. I don't recall tasting anything close to the delicate yet vibrant taste. When we returned to Alagna there was bad news about the Space Cadet. The engine had run out of oil and seized up—it was history. I felt pretty bad for Armin. His guide's salary didn't leave much margin for purchasing new cars.

In a borrowed VW bus, we motored the one and a half hours to Milan, accompanied by the Sesia River rushing off the slopes of Monte Rosa. I was told it's a great whitewater challenge for kayakers. There were many homes and small villages all along its banks. Here, as in so much of Europe, space was at a premium and it's not surprising why Europeans are so fascinated by the wide-open spaces of our American West. As I left Milan by jet, I expected I'd be back to climb in the Alps again soon. Armin and I had talked about climbing the legendary Matterhorn, not by the tourist route, but one of the moderate ridge classics like the Zmutt or the Liongrat. But as I write this, many years later, I think with regret that dream may never be realized.

Chapter 11
Down Canyon

One of the best paying professions is getting ahold of pieces of country in your mind, learning their smell and their moods, sorting out the pieces of a view, deciding what grows there and there and why, how many steps that hill will take, where this creek winds and where it meets the other one below, what elevation timberline is now, whether you can walk this reef at low tide or have to climb around, which contour lines on a map mean better cliffs or mountains. This is the best kind of ownership, and the most permanent.
—Jerry and Rennie Russel from On the Loose

I like geography best, he said, because your mountains and rivers know the secret. Pay no attention to boundaries.
—Brian Andreas

The canyon is close to town and at the same time big, wild and unknown. Many people have been in there over the years, yet you hardly ever see another soul. Logged and explored for mining purposes in the distant past and once an early municipal water source, you can often find the old water pipes, broken and dry. Yet even now, only a tiny fraction of the local population knows anything about it. For me, it had become a retreat, my own de facto private park. Admittedly, all of it is private property but the landowners rarely, if ever, venture in. It is pristine territory, composed of rugged and steeply angled slopes with few trails. Cover consists of mixed woodland forest, with alder, bay, and spice bush by the creek, tan oak, black oak, and madrone on the flats, a few solitary ponderosa pine and giant Douglas fir on the steep slopes. I relished the wilderness being so close by and considered myself a guardian of the canyon.

The few that venture in here are often young, high-school-age boys looking to burn some youthful energy. They do not have the value of years yet to cherish the place the way I do. Sometimes there would be trash and the more ominous fire rings left on their rare overnight stays. I've carried out their beer cans and plastic wrap and scattered their soot-blackened circle of rocks to make it clean again. In the days when the landowner lived nearby, he rebuilt the old trail, placed some arrow signs, and left a picnic table at an overlook. The table eventually disintegrated and I found it one day pitched into the creek two hundred feet below. It took several trips to carry the boards out on my back.

Once I found the remains of a big marijuana operation in an outrageously remote location after it had been busted by the feds. An acre of undergrowth had been cut then piled in a circular brush fence to screen it from any passersby. Hundreds of plastic pots, clothing rags, and food cans labeled in Spanish were strewn everywhere. It was a mess and all I could take out were two 500-foot coils of half-inch irrigation hose, still bound by the original bands. I removed them one at a time by tying a short rope around the coils and dragging them a mile to the road.

After winter windstorms, I cleared the trails of deadfall. Once a fallen tree took out part of the trail. I repaired the spot with fill dirt making a rolling dip to divert water off the trail and covered it with fir needles and oak leaves. Some years later it is still holding. Others own the land but, in a way, it has been mine, because I love it more and know it better than anyone alive.

Back in the days when I lived at the historic resort down-canyon, we had permission to collect firewood anywhere on the property to heat our drafty, one-room cabins, originally built for summer use. That meant hundreds of acres of wild land was ours to explore.

Chapter 11

One quiet autumn day, I followed a tributary of the main creek as far as it went, looking for the source spring that flowed all summer, even in the worst drought years. Not far from the main stem, the canyon of the tributary narrows where five, paternoster pools are found, each one unique, each one beautiful. The canyon slopes are steep and direct sunlight rarely penetrates. Much farther up, after two hours of toil, are precipitate-rimmed pools like at Havasu in the Grand Canyon. Five-finger ferns adorn and frame the falls so I named it the Hanging Gardens. Many hours later on my search, soon after sighting a red fox slipping behind a log, I found the source, bubbling out of the ground entirely without fanfare. Above that the streambed was dry, and the canyon rose steeply to its finish on the ridgetop. If anyone had been in there in the last fifty years then no evidence remained. I returned near dark on that short autumn day and though I was much younger then, the muscles in my upper legs were sore for days.

However, even by the late 1990s, after fifteen years of day-hiking, overnights, and skinny-dipping the best pools, I had never fully explored the main creek. The lower part I knew well, a good two miles of it—every pool and fall along the way, every tree fallen to form a cross-stream bridge, every alluvial bench comfortable for a camp-out, secure from the lights and noise of the valley. Each year, tens of thousands of ladybugs converge in early summer at the streams' confluence for what scientists call a reproductive diapause. The ladybugs (really beetles) cover the rocks, tree roots, and stream banks thickly, one on top of another, several layers deep, like snakes in a pit. Their return each year was reminiscent of a steelhead run, an ancient homecoming. Whenever I was lucky enough to be there at this event, I stepped around them as best I could.

Double Falls

Farther upstream you pass the tributary and follow the main canyon to where it narrows to reveal two waterfalls, the first twenty, the second forty feet high. To access the second pool requires climbing skills. Eons of rushing water have polished the rock smooth but left some indentations good for the palm or a big toe. With the right pressure, balance, and friction, using these miniature dishes in the rock, ascent is possible. The pool is wide, deep, and cold at all times of the year. An image in the rock that appears in a certain light and at the right time of day lent the name I gave it—Panther Pool. By late summer only a trickle of water shimmies down the falls and an ascent up the left side of the forty-foot falls becomes possible. The holds are bigger and

Chapter 11

square-cut for the first half, but higher up the holds are water-smoothed. Again, a climber must use friction to surmount the lip. Only once had I hiked above this obstacle, finding massive, jumbled boulders in the streambed. I assumed at that high point that the major obstacles were over and further progress up the stream to the ridgetop would be easier. It proved, like many assumptions, to be wrong. In the summer of 2000, I made plans to explore the entire canyon.

John, 70 years young at the time, was a close friend and mentor. Retired from psychiatric doctor duties, he was a local legend in folk-dancing circles and non-impact aerobics and a great lover of gardens. He had accompanied my wife, stepdaughter, and me on a High Sierra trip, and when the horse packer failed to meet us on the day of our return, we made the fourteen-mile trek out on foot. Despite his age, I trusted John's conditioning.

Our other companion was Peggy, about fifty at the time, a folk dancer also and a former backpacker. Her husband had deserted her in mid-life, a fact she let be known with a quiet sigh of exasperation. In her former life, she had lived a 'back to the land' existence. She still lived on a few acres, growing two greenhouses of orchids as a side business. Enviably, Peggy was one of those special people who retained conditioning without training. I trusted her ability too.

Without technical climbing experience, however, my friends were placing a great deal of trust in me, more than they knew perhaps, on this unknown canyoneering adventure. There were no guidebooks to consult, no internet to trawl, and no one I knew could tell me about the upper canyon. I brought a lot of enthusiasm and a lot of experience in the outdoors. Still, we'd be in a remote, rugged area where rescue might not arrive on the day it was needed.

The idea I'd hatched and convinced my friends as a good idea was this: We'd leave a car at the takeout, drive a second car nearly to the ridgetop 2,000 vertical feet above the valley, park at the county road's end, and start hiking. For two miles we would cross private vineyard land, then connect with the canyon and begin our descent of over 1,500 feet down the unexplored stream canyon, until reaching my previous high point. From there it should be smooth sailing.

The plan was to stick entirely to the stream or its near banks, knowing that in late summer water levels are low and that rocks showing above water line would be dry and good for rock hopping. My biggest worry was the presence of high, unknown drop-offs. To save weight I brought only 50 feet of climbing rope, some nylon slings, and aluminum alloy carabiners, plus a belay device to lower my partners down the waterfalls. Once they were safely down, I would down-climb these falls without a rope.

The late August morning dawned clear and warm with none of the refreshing coolness preferable at that time of day. It would be downright hot later on and we started early. Leaving Peggy's vintage Volvo at the takeout under a shady redwood tree, my Nissan truck took us back to town then up a curvy, windy, and beautiful two-lane county road. We passed hillside vineyards bordered by olive trees, encircled by towering Douglas firs on all sides. It was easy to imagine the majestic forest once entire, now replaced by vines.

I punched the time button on my radio and it read 7 AM, a great start. Each of us shouldered our daypacks full of water and food, mine a bit heavier with the climbing equipment. The air was even hotter up here due to the temperature inversion.

We quickly ascended the winery service road and came upon a view of extensive vineyards. All this had been gently sloped forested lands until the 1980s when vineyard conversion took place. It would be prudent to get the first section done at a fast clip. We had not asked permission to cross this area but were pretty sure the landowners wouldn't object. Tearing across private land with an all-terrain vehicle is not tolerated, but a hiker

Chapter 11

leaves little trace. It was only in the recent past that all these lands were unfenced and neighbors commonly rode horses freely across another's property. Nevertheless, we had chosen an early Sunday morning when vineyard operations would be quiet. We preferred to pass through unnoticed.

Our conversation was low but upbeat and full of contained excitement as we made jaunty progress along the vineyard avenues. Several small houses belonging to employees were passed, but we neither saw nor heard anyone at this hour. At the end of the properties, we looked west to the ridgetop, where the creek began as an unassuming dry defile, a simple rift in the wall of the watershed. From where we stood, however, the creek had widened and was already carrying out its creekly duties as we entered the shade. The alder trees filtered and toned down the sunlight and heat, and suddenly we were in a different world. Having been exposed and vulnerable out in that viney world, we now relaxed into our element and silently congratulated each other on the completion of the first segment.

We stopped for food and drink and to assess our situation. In the vineyard the air temperature had already been in the high eighties, but here it was at least ten degrees cooler. The boulder-strewn creek was inviting us to explore its alternating pools, small falls, and cascades descending at an easy gradient. We were at home. Sometimes we jumped from rock to dry rock, making sure of each foot placement, but often walked along the banks when a pool was wide and deep. I made a game of using balancing skills to keep my shoes dry but John and Peggy relished in wading frequently in the cool waters.

The lead hiker would often hear the plop of a Pacific tree frog making the leap from shore to pool. If your eyes were quick you might see it swim for the bottom through expanding ripples and quickly bury itself in the sand or mud. Dragonflies sporting orange and black or blue and gray colors would shoot downstream on their own commuter highway, then some minutes later make the return trip at the same speed. Their smaller relatives, the Damsel Fly, stood delicately poised on exposed streambed rocks. When the light shone through their wings, the fine web-like structure was revealed, as beautiful as any cathedral stained-glass window. I looked for the appearance of the water ouzel or dipper, named for its characteristic bobbing habit. It is rare in the county and only three sightings are known, one of them right here in this watershed.

The Great Blue Heron sometimes shows up in the lower canyon. Coming around a bend in the creek I have startled his concentration and, with surprising speed for a big bird, he would take off with a great beating of wings to negotiate his way through the tree overstory. The species most conspicuously absent is the steelhead trout. The forty-foot falls below us prevents their migration upstream but even in the lower stretches, the stream is empty. It is hoped a fish ladder installed by the California Department of Fish and Wildlife will encourage their return.

Those who haven't ventured beyond the pavement may be surprised how wild these stream canyons of California's North Bay still are. Once on the lower main stem, only ten minutes from the road, I discovered the remains of a freshly killed fawn on a large alluvial bench above the creek. All that was left were the skull, four tiny hooves, and the internal organs, still bright and glistening in the sun. Mountain lions take out the internal organs to preserve the meat. I was shaken by this discovery, and although it was a sunny, summer day the woods seemed to darken a bit. I listened intently over my quickening heart rate and tried to sense whether the lion would return. Picking up a stout stick I moved on cautiously.

Upstream was a second, larger fresh carcass, perhaps the mother of the fawn. It had been dragged to a small bench above the creek, where many bones were scattered about. I imagined the deer were thirsty so had taken the risk of coming down to

Chapter 11

the creek where the lion had killed them.

We continued our steady and pleasant progress downstream as a rhythm and a knowingness came to our movements. This movement from rock to rock was pure pleasure. We made our choices in successive split seconds, letting the body take total control. The mind is too slow for this work. By late morning this riparian corridor had become the extent of awareness, where we remained immune to rising temperatures in the unshaded world.

None of us wore a watch, so we reached a hunger consensus and chose a flat rock from which to dip our feet and to have a proper lunch. During the last hour, I had been scanning ahead through breaks in the canopy for familiar landmarks. To my surprise, there had been none. I was starting to feel the first twinges of anxiety. There is an odd dichotomy that adventurers feel on outings like this one. We long for new places and experiences, then start worrying we've overreached. So far John and Peggy seem untroubled by worries so I kept the feeling to myself.

We pushed on following the stream in its steady but unspectacular downward progress. There was no evidence of human passage. Occasionally we saw the unwelcome sight of vineyard debris such as plastic irrigation hose, washed down in the last flood. If trash was small enough it went into our packs. The sun passed its zenith and still no recognizable landmarks appeared. How long *was* this canyon? I told myself to exercise patience. One can't gauge stream miles by trail miles. As the crow flies, we had only four miles of watershed to cover. Two miles an hour is a good speed on a hiking trail. Here, however, our pace was only a half-mile each hour. Patience.

Suddenly it became brighter as the canopy thinned, the stream widened, rocks flattened, and we came to an overlook. A slight breeze ruffled the alder leaves. John was the first to walk out to the end of the smooth, flat rocks where he stopped to peer over.

"Oh my God!" was all he said.

I had sat down to take a drink. Peggy joined him, she leaned over cautiously and repeated his words—"Oh my God!" and said nothing more. They certainly had my curiosity piqued. Both seemed a bit stunned. I walked out to join the two and gazed down into the abyss. Unaware of the repetition, I echoed their exact words.

Below me in a tight and rock-bound chasm was a waterfall of over a hundred feet, falling in three distinct segments. The first third began as a cascade down a steeply inclined waterslide. The second segment, shunted by contours of the rock, took a distinct turn to the right. The last third fell sheer into a large pool fifty feet across. I stood there on the lip, stunned for several minutes saying nothing, and understood only one thing—that my precious plan to follow this creek to the bottom was looking impossible. Our rope was far too short and down-climbing would be suicide. Also, there was no room in this sharp defile to down-climb left or right of the falls. The adventure seemed to be over. I guessed we were more than halfway through the canyon. To retrace our steps now would be possible but time consuming and worst, horribly disheartening. This was not the way it was supposed to be. It was meant to end in the cool forest at the bottom, not a walk back through vineyards where the air temperatures were now over 100° F.

Finally, avoiding a mild panic, I saw a possible alternative just ten yards back from the falls. The right-hand slope was not so severe as the left side and the angle eased higher up. No one wanted to return so we resolved to try it. I had climbed plenty of crappy looking hillsides before but John, even if he had in his youth, was starting his eighth decade. Roping up would not be safe without any decent anchors above, so in the end, I simply climbed directly behind John to be sure he didn't slip on the loose hillside. Through this most dangerous part of the trip, John was uncomplaining. Eventually, the slope lessened and after much uphill cross-country travel, fighting brush and downed

Chapter 11

logs, we found a minor, dry streambed back to the main stem. The detour took over an hour of intense effort.

Back on track, Peggy and I left John to a well-deserved nap and went the short distance upstream to view what turns out to be the highest (and virtually unknown) waterfall in the county. From this vantage, I confirmed that the falls were un-climbable without a full complement of climbing gear. By wordless consent, we slipped into the refreshing pool sans clothing. Tired but relieved to be below this massive obstacle, a nagging thought popped into my mind to trouble the idyllic moment—was there another falls like it below?

Peggy and I found John nearly asleep but game to go on. The gradient was steep with massive boulders to climb over, under, or between. It was finally here, in this stretch, that I recognized my high point from the past. With great relief I let my friends know we were on familiar ground from now on. Time seemed to pass more quickly and soon we came to the lip of the forty-foot falls. The only anchor I could find was a small, multi-branched cottonwood tree. Wrapping the thin trunks with a large nylon sling, I then attached two carabiners. While Peggy and John slipped into their harnesses, I tied the rope into my own harness and then to the anchor carabiners with a figure-eight knot. I stood forward of the anchor, tied the other end to John, and said:

"Ok, all you have to do is walk backwards."

"Walk backwards?"

"Uh-huh, I'll take all the weight."

John's transition from the flat edge to the vertical face would be the hardest.

"Keep your body at a right angle to the rock and relax."

John had never done anything like this in his life. Eyeing the thin cottonwood trunks, I braced my feet on a rock for extra security. John did just fine until the bottom, where he lost his concentration, slipped on a wet rock and plunged into the pool, coming up laughing.

"Keep going, there's another ten feet or so."

He unclipped the figure-eight knot from the locking carabiner attached to his harness. I pulled up the rope and repeated the process for Peggy. She went down without incident and then it was my turn. I unclipped the rope and tossed it down to have Peggy coil. It was no use to me since I'd need double the amount of rope to rappel and retrieve it. I could have rappelled the single strand and left it in place but leaving trash went against my ethics. I put the slings and carabiners in my pack, faced rockwards, and began some delicate, thin face climbing. The hardest part is at the start where one risks a fall that might end in the pool, or it might mean glancing off the rock first. Best not think about that. Very methodically and slowly I made sure of each hold. Then I was down. A second shorter section required the same techniques but with far less danger.

A great relief came over our party as the last technical difficulties were passed. We had done it. And with lots of warm daylight left, Peggy and I could not resist another swim. Once again, we shed our clothes and slipped into the cooling water of a small but deep hole, home to several Pacific tree frogs. John took another well-deserved nap. The afternoon sun rays shone brightly through Douglas fir trees, roots bracing against the pull of the steep canyon walls. With the heat gradually softening, and the sun in our faces, we felt the shocking contrast of cold water on our warm, naked skin. Then resting, we sat next to each other on a log, dangling our feet and drawing water striders to our toes. I felt the exquisite, casual touch of her upper arm on mine. Neither of us wanted to move, a perfect moment of repose and reflection, quiet conversation, and the murmuring of the stream.

Finally, it was time to go. Peggy and I skipped from rock to rock, our steps still light and fluid. John happily and exhaustedly splashed through each and every pool, just like a school kid. We passed the tributary coming in from the right. Here, the multi-

Chapter 11

colored rocks, the exposed roots of sycamores and alders, and the mossy riverbanks held this year's swarm of resting ladybugs. We crossed the alluvial bench where the fawn had been killed just a year past, no trace left now. Around the familiar river bends we continued, past the native bunch grasses that green each summer in mid-creek. Two downed redwoods that span the creek at eye level sheltered a pool that would, ten years hence, became a refuge for a trapped steelhead waiting patiently for the winter rains. At last, the bridge came into view and the road passing over it. We came to the Volvo, and leaned against it, reluctant to get inside. Overhead, a massive grandfather redwood towered protectively, and the deepening shadows gave us their evening benediction.

> *Some twenty years after this day fire swept through the canyon, sparing nothing, destroying everything, the drier upper slopes as well as the riparian vegetation in the creek bottom. I didn't and couldn't bear to return to my refuge for nearly a year. When I did, there were some signs of rebirth, redwoods sprouting their needle leaves directly out of friable and blackened trunks, the growth of perennial grasses and flowers. I came upon a pier block foundation of an old cabin, perhaps a logger's, hidden by thickets of spice bush for a century. But it will take decades, generations, for the forest to regain its former glory, certainly not in my lifetime. This then, is a requiem for a place no one knew.*

Chapter 12
Half Dome: Fifth Time is the Charm

People say that what we're all seeking is a meaning for life. I don't think that's what we're really seeking. I think that what we're seeking is an experience of being alive, so that our life experiences on the purely physical plane will have resonances within our own innermost being and reality, so that we actually feel the rapture of being alive.
—Joseph Campbell

When I think about how all this business started, this obsession with ascending big rock walls, a typical Santa Barbara spring day comes to mind, clear and warm, in 1977. Warren, my lanky, long-haired climbing partner and I were walking along upper State Street in the Samarkand district nearby where I lived. We were headed for some forgotten destination when a new acquaintance, Doug Hsu, approached. We'd seen him at Gibraltar Rock, the area's main climbing crag in upper Rattlesnake canyon in the mountains north of town. Doug was a natural and unschooled talent who began climbing alone because he knew no other climbers.

Gibraltar's classic testpiece is a severely overhanging crack called The Nose. Neither Warren nor I could climb it at the time, even with the help of a top rope. Yet Doug had done it several times alone, with only his climbing shoes and a chalk bag. On one occasion that he was climbing solo and unroped, he lost concentration and fell thirty feet into a steeply sloping, boulder choked gully—and then walked away with only a few bruises and a sprained ankle.

The day we met he was psyched.

"Fitch and I climbed Half Dome last weekend!"

Chuck Fitch, another local climber, was possibly a greater natural talent than Hsu. Doug was referring to the *uberwall* known as the Northwest Face of Half Dome, over 2,000 feet of vertical granite—the iconic symbol of Yosemite National Park.

"You guys should set your sights, it's totally doable. It's practically all free climbing with lots of beautiful cracks and no hanging belays."

Doug contrasted this wall with El Capitan, the other iconic big stone in Yosemite. El Cap is so steep and smooth that aid climbing is often required and hanging belays abound. Half Dome's famous passages that he described were familiar to me. In my college days at UCSB there wasn't a single piece of climbing literature in the seven-story library that escaped my notice. The writings of Royal Robbins, Tom Frost, Chuck Pratt, Steve Roper, Alan Steck, and other Yosemite Golden Age pioneers were scripture. But now I was hearing it from someone who had just been there. Hsu described the Robbins Traverse (a varied-width 300-foot long horizontal ledge that partially disappeared one day in 2015), Big Sandy Ledge (where a comfortable night could be spent) as well as the awesome Zig Zags (three back-to-back vertical to overhanging cracks requiring gymnastic abilities, probably beyond our free climbing skills).

"And Thank God Ledge man, it's so amazing, less than a foot wide, forty feet long on this completely blank face, with 2,000 feet of air straight to the bottom!"

His descriptions were jangling, electrifying every nerve in our bodies.

"I know you guys can do it."

We appreciated his faith in us, his encouragement for an adventure we'd fantasized about but not had the vision to materialize. And it turned out he'd done it all on that sprained ankle—the so-called Death Slabs approach from Mirror Lake,

Chapter 12

the long climb itself, and then the brutal pounding descent, 4,000 feet of it to the Valley floor. If he could do it injured then couldn't we in full health?

I didn't know how Warren was feeling at this moment, but underneath my surface enthusiasm, my stomach felt like a field of volcanic fumaroles. My partner and I had been climbing for six years now, but most of our climbs had been short ones. We hadn't even finished Yosemite's moderate classic Royal Arches the previous summer. Blasted by a 105° F heatwave, we'd had to descend from two-thirds up the sixteen-hundred-foot route.

But still, at twenty-five, we were in the bloom of youth and feeling virtually immortal. The bulk of our potential hadn't been tapped yet. As Doug limped off down State Street, the seed had been planted and only a month later we traveled to Yosemite to make a first attempt.

Once in a while, a climb will just have it out for you, repel all your attempts, throw one guise after another to keep you away. Half Domes' Northwest Face had put a hex on me and all my attempts to court her were rebuffed. That first attempt in May of 1977 saw record—sometimes torrential—rains for the whole month. We spent all our time waiting in the community building at Camp Curry with other frustrated hikers and climbers. We drove home without even getting close to rock. In 1980, a year's plan came to naught when I came down with a bad flu-bug days before the big climb. In 1981, another plan was foiled when a partner badly sprained an ankle falling off the infamous mantle move on Nutcracker. Three plans, three failures and I'd still never reached the base of Half Dome.

Then I met Mark. He was fit, strong, and motivated, and so Half Dome was back on the front burner. We were planning the climb for August of 1986. On the surface all was well and preparations were moving forward. Yet popping up uninvited were foreboding feelings, premonitions, and singular bad dreams at night. I shook them off. Friends and family knew all about the big plans, but inside I was more anxious than usual.

As I drove into Yosemite Valley I found this note on Mark's vehicle—"Ken, I'm up on the DNB (Direct North Buttress of Middle Cathedral Rock) meet you tomorrow at 3 PM, Camp Curry." The next day he was flush with excitement, confidence, and success on a difficult, sometimes dangerous big route. He had met a party by chance who needed a third climber and jumped at the opportunity.

"Half Dome will be a cruise, I've got the hauling system down!" For the two years I'd known Mark, he had been the low-key, less experienced one in our partnership, always taking cues from me. Now he was bursting with a new energy and a new personality. I didn't know how to handle the new Mark. Normally, he approached climbs soberly, but his enthusiasm now knew no bounds.

With a hundred pounds of gear, we took the long and punishing Mist Trail to Half Dome's east side and spent the night. The next day we traversed cross-country around the north side to the base. By the time we'd filled water bottles at the spring and readied everything, it was 3 PM. Immediately we got off-route and by 5 PM we had completed only one pitch. For the first time I could remember, Mark and I were not getting along. Nothing felt right and I told Mark my heart and mind were not in it. Perhaps I would have felt different in the morning. But Mark surprised me by packing up and leaving for the Valley floor immediately.

That was the end of my fourth attempt, but much worse it proved to be the end of our partnership. I spent a few days in the Valley doing touristy things and decompressing, numbing out all the complex emotions. I returned home to my little retreat cabin in the woods. A fourth failure was not easy to take. I would soon call it the Half Dome Abortion.

2 AM—I woke with a start in the pitch black with heart pounding. No, *hammering*. Fast, hard. My chest felt like it could

Chapter 12

burst. I sat up scared and alone. Heart attack? There was no history in my family. *Boom, boom boom!* —my heart was out of control. What could bring on this sudden-onset malfunction? Shakily, I got out of bed. Moving helped, but a dreadful anxiety gripped my heart. Gotta do something. I opened the cabin door—outside it was a moonless night, no sounds from the few occupied cabins nearby. My ten-speed bicycle leaned against one wall. I brought it inside, took the thing apart, cleaned it, restored it. Hours passed but by first light fear still hung around like death.

I called a hotline. A man answered and I told him a long story, the ten-year dream, the failures, my hammering heart. Did I have some disease? Should I see a doctor? Although he knew nothing about climbing, he understood.

"Ken, you need to get back on the rock immediately. Get back on the horse after the fall. This is nothing but a panic attack."

Panic attack, me? All this was psychosomatic?

Feeling tremendous relief, though still somewhat shaky, I enjoyed the sunrise and breakfast. The phone rang. Who could that be at 7 AM?

"Hey, my name's Armin. I saw your letter to the editor in *Climbing* magazine. I live nearby. Want to do some climbing today?"

What were the chances of that, the timing of that phone call? If I wanted proof of destiny or fate, there was no need to look further.

We climbed at a local crag that day, and I could see that Armin was a natural talent. But when he free-soloed a 75-foot overhanging route it was obvious he was in another league. That was the start of not only a long friendship but eventually, years later, my ticket to unlocking the barriers to Half Dome. Barriers that were many and varied, both physical and psychological, that would all need surmounting before the dream could be realized.

The most daunting of these challenges came many years later, in the fall of 1996 when Mac, my new climbing partner and I were headed to Pinnacles for a climbing trip. On a whim I impulsively proposed changing course to hike/climb up Yosemite's highest peak, Mt. Lyell. It was a foolish move. In below freezing temperatures we covered 25 miles in a long round trip day. I'd bruised my tailbone falling on the glacier and limped badly the last two miles. We hadn't even won the peak, turned back by bad weather. Coupled with a work injury two days later, overstressed nerves in my back and left leg snapped. A frustrating case of sciatica lasted four months. Depression deepened into the winter as the doctors could do nothing for it. Finally, a friend recommended alternative therapy, and a Hanna Somatics practitioner cured it one treatment. It's never returned.

To be free of chronic pain is like having a veil lifted from your eyes. I was ecstatic, now 47 years old, and realized that not many more years of really hard climbing were left. If I wanted to fulfill my dream of the Northwest Face of Half Dome then it was now or never. A grand period of big wall climbing was thus ushered in, and by the summer of 2002, I was psychologically and physically as fit as I'd ever be. And for what was now the *fifth* time, I was part of a plan to climb Half Dome.

The previous winter and spring Mac and I had trained at the gym three times a week and spent many weekends in Tahoe doing our big-wall training regimen, climbing at least a thousand feet per day. In June 2002 we met Armin in the Valley. Our approach march was from Mirror Lake, up the Death Slabs, the same approach Chuck Fitch and Doug Hsu had taken 25 years earlier. In the early dawn we had to strip to our underwear and cross frigid Tenaya Creek barefoot with our packs over our heads. Fortunately, the crossing was brief and the water barely moving.

The Death Slabs presented numerous difficulties, like narrow, steep, and exposed trails, slick granite slabs running with

Chapter 12

water, and steep rock steps that sometimes had fixed ropes you could ascend by 'batman' or jumar techniques. In about three hours we approached the great shadowed wall. Here several missile rocks lay strewn about, either in or near small craters caused by their long fall from above. We donned our helmets for this part and passed with relief through the danger zone quickly and came to the start of the Northwest Face route. I had been here 16 years before in quite different circumstances. This time I felt relaxed and confident.

From the base of Half Dome, the vast gray prominence totally dominated our vision. The width of the Dome was just as impressive as the height, perhaps six to eight football fields stretched end to end. Mac rested while Armin and I fixed the first three pitches, wonderful free climbing, including a bottomless chimney slot that took a struggle to wiggle into. Then our work was done for the day and we sat back in comfort and enjoyed a meal as the slanting rays of the sun raked across awesome Tenaya Canyon 2,000 feet below. Two young climbers showed up about 6 PM and asked if they could jumar our fixed ropes in their attempt to climb it in a day. We thought it odd they would start so late but gave our assent. Near dark, two Spaniards also intent on the climb showed up with very light packs and we conversed around a campfire, Armin, with his fluent Italian being close enough to Spanish, was able to communicate. Meanwhile, the climbers above returned by 9 PM via headlamp and, without a word, disappeared down the trail.

We slammed a cold breakfast and were jumaring the fixed ropes by dawn. We had first dibs on the route, being ahead of the Spaniards, but Armin assured them that we'd be fast. Indeed, the three of us—even with a haul sack of 50 pounds—stayed ahead of the pair the entire day. Armin's first big wall had been this very climb at 16 years of age. When his partner had a mental breakdown, Armin literally tied him to the haul sack and hauled him up the remainder of the way.

No Mere Pastime

Our process was such—Armin would lead, I'd follow in the free climbing style and clean gear, and Mac would jumar most pitches and free the haul sack if it got stuck. The same team that had done Leaning Tower and El Cap was working like clockwork. The fourth pitch I remember as quite strenuous, what climbers call old-school 5.9, usually meaning harder. About a third of the way up is the Robbins Traverse, which involved dragging the haul sack for 300 feet, a wearisome experience punctuated by a thin and exposed move with the risk of a pendulum fall.

We stopped at pitch 11 for a bite to eat and concurred with the guidebook that the cramped and down-sloping ledge would make a lousy bivouac for any sized party. A remarkable 200 feet of wide chimneys followed, capped by an overhanging finish while the haul sack went up the smooth face on the outside. We were moving so fast that I ran out of gas and had to beg my partners to stop and pull out a Clif bar for me. A lieback/jam crack was more strenuous than I expected and then we hauled up onto Big Sandy Ledge, 18 pitches from the base with plenty of daylight to spare.

Here, another surprise presented itself. For 25 years I had anticipated this bivouac and imagined a large, spacious, sandy, flat-floored enclosure, something like Dinner Ledge on the South Face of Washington Column. The Supertopo guidebook calls it a "deluxe bivy for four". Huh. What you have is a smooth, 15-foot-long ledge that contours concavely like a warped plank. It's just wide enough to hold a human body and only long enough to hold *three* comfortably. Not that I was complaining—it was just neither big nor sandy.

A fixed rope along its length allowed us to move freely about with a sliding daisy chain attached to our harnesses. Alpenglow flooded the Dome and Tenaya Canyon, now 3,000 feet below, and the great El Cap-like face of Mt. Watkins, nearly as massive as its famous counterpart.

Chapter 12

We were having a cold-dinner feast enjoying the view and the company when the first of the Spaniards appeared. Soon his companion arrived, and they occupied some lumpy, sharp-edged ledges above us. We had extra food and they were happy to supplement their meager fare. Then they retired quickly. We got into our sleeping bags, looking like three down-enveloped sardines in a granite tin. Facing the wall was claustrophobic so I turned facing out. Without moving an eyelash I could see straight down the dead-vertical 1,500-foot drop to the base of the Dome, the Death Slabs below that, and then Mirror Lake another 2,000 feet beyond. My daisy chain tether was taut, secured to the anchor, and my harness was fixed by two locking carabiners.

I awakened once during the night to see great clouds of cumulus to the east and worried since we had no raingear. Other than that, I slept well. We learned later that it had snowed on Mt. Whitney.

At dawn, the sound of a dog barking traveled all the way up from a campground in Yosemite Valley. The clouds were gone but it was cold as we patiently let the Spaniards start out first. They had endured a miserable night with only light coverings to keep them warm. We let them get well ahead. Now, the long-anticipated Zig Zag pitches were just above. They presented a crazy aspect on this vertical wall, not only darting from left to right and back again, but alternately overhanging and flipping back to vertical or less for a full three hundred feet. We used a combination of free and aid climbing techniques on this famous passage.

Armin on the Zig Zags, NW face of Half Dome, Yosemite

Chapter 12

The summit overhangs loomed over us like tiered layer cake. As far as I know, they have never been climbed. Ever since the first ascent party had discovered Thank God Ledge, everyone has taken it. It is one of the most amazing escape routes in the climbing world, easy but so exposed that it gives even great climbers pause. There is nothing to break the fall of a dropped object until it hits the base. This is the key to the highway, the Yellow Brick Road, Wall Street for acrophobics. It is a classic exfoliating slab, slowly detaching itself from the wall. Someday it will disappear. Armin was able to walk across the ledge the whole way. I used several techniques—walking, crawling on hands and knees, hand traversing at the narrowest part, then back to an upright position where the ledge widened at the end.

But the climb was not over. Above us was the technical crux of the whole route, if free climbed it goes at 5.12. Armin used aid techniques, several A3 hook moves on broken bolt studs. And then the rest was a low-angled ramp. On top, we greeted friends and family who had hiked up the back side. In the final tally, I was able to free climb 22 of the 24 pitches on the route, and it felt good for a guy over the half-century mark.

I reflected on my first time up Half Dome 31 years ago, just months before my climbing days had begun. The cable route had been a psychological, rather than a physical, challenge. I remember someone was throwing a frisbee off the top. I don't think anyone realized the danger to climbers below. My hiking partner recommended I crawl out on the Visor, the diving board-like slab on top of the great overhangs. I lay prone gazing down the mind-numbing drop to Mirror Lake, petrified and exhilarated simultaneously. The thought of climbing this incomprehensible wall never entered my mind. My strongest impression had been how easy it would be to slip off the perch and do a final swan-dive into oblivion. I never forgot that feeling. Sometimes I would imagine a future dystopic world, no longer worth living in, and returning to this airy perch to go out in style.

*Ken hand traversing Thank God Ledge,
NW face of Half Dome
Photo by Armin Fisher*

Chapter 12

Unlike most of my other big-wall climbs, on this one there were no struggles to speak of, no sleepless night before the big push. Having climbed El Capitan earlier, you might almost think it was anticlimactic. But that's far from the truth. There was great joy in the fulfillment of this lifetime dream. All the years of dreaming, scheming, and struggle were behind me. The broken plans, the Half Dome Abortion of 1986, the lost partnership, the injuries, and anguish, it had all been worth it. A great healing took place for me that day.

The summit photo shows the three of us hugging, grinning ear to ear. My sister Leslie, among the party to meet us on top, said she'd never seen me climb before. But Armin and Mac had to scoot, having business at home. We scampered down the cable route, which felt low angle by comparison. I camped out in Little Yosemite for a night with the rest of the party. On the way down the Mist Trail, Phil embarrassed me by announcing to all and sundry we passed that I had just climbed the great Northwest Face. At the trailhead to greet me were my Mom and other sister who gave their congratulations.

In the days and weeks that followed I felt a deep energy shift inside me. It was like a motor whose transmission had been torqued in the red zone for years, now throttled back to a comfortable cruising speed. Something profound but subtle had changed, and I knew I could never train so hard, or desire so fiercely in the pursuit of a goal. In the months that followed I would wonder where my drive to climb, 30 years of it, had gone. What would take its place? I would feel a vacuum out ahead of me for some time.

Gradually it became unnecessary to have the next goal and the next to satisfy me. Not that I would stop climbing altogether. There were still some wildfires to snuff. The momentum of a lifetime would carry me up some big routes, including the Steck/Salathe on Sentinel, which proved to be my big-wall swansong. After that my life changed radically. At 54 my body was telling me that it wasn't immortal after all. To paraphrase Maurice Herzog, the first person up Annapurna—there are other Half Domes in the lives of men and women.

Chapter 13
Jammin' Glacier

[Red Bus] Drivers were paid at rates substantially higher than most others park employees, at one time earning $100 a month compared to $30 paid to bellhops, considered a top hotel position because of the opportunity to earn tips. At East Glacier drivers had separate housing and their own canteen, ...reputed to serve the best staff meals in the park. This...reinforced the belief that drivers were Glacier's pampered elite. Male staff sometimes took an intense dislike to these traveling Don Juans, who traipsed in and out every few days wooing 'their' girls.
—From *Glacier Park Inc. Tour/Shuttle Driver Commentary and Reference Manual* Formatted and Edited by Richard Bond GPI Transportation Manager

It sounded like an idyllic way to spend the summer of 2004—four months living and working in Montana's Glacier National Park, driving and leading tours on the famous Red Bus. I'd visited Glacier before and thought it the best the West had to offer. I let myself get carried away by my wife's enthusiasm for a change in our routine. We applied online early in the year and by February I got a call from the boss. He was impressed that I had years of experience using a commercial driver's license, even when he found out it wasn't passengers I transported but wine grapes. The salary came to about seven bucks an hour, paltry compensation for the responsibility of people's lives. Fortunately, it wasn't the money I needed. I packed some blank journals thinking it might make a good story.

But how often do the best-laid plans work out the way you

want? My first day at the park was a barometer reading in more ways than one.

Sleep was elusive on this first night in East Glacier. I was squeezed into a short and narrow single bed, my feet touched the bottom board, and the thin mattress sank below the level of the frame. The only other furniture in a room only slightly larger than a walk-in closet was a table and chair. A light burned brightly in the hallway outside the room. To block the glare, I spread a cheap curtain across the window and secured it with a safety pin someone else had used before. Footsteps echoed loudly on the wooden hallway, doors slammed, a TV hummed next door. Gilligan was getting the best of the Skipper. My body throbbed with that peculiar, unsatisfactory fatigue you get from a day of plane flights, airport hassles, and no exercise. Around midnight, as some of these noises faded, I had become aware of someone down below pounding on pipes with a hammer or rubber mallet. At regular thirty-second intervals, there was a one-two beat, *thump-thump, thump-thump*. I thought about going down the stairwell to complain but it was cold, I'd have lost the warmth of my sleeping bag, and I was too damn tired to move…

Breakfast was in the EDR (employee dining room for the neophyte—everything was shortened to acronyms when you worked for GPI (Glacier Park Incorporated), the concession owned by Viad Corporation that operated the great lodges of the park). Over a bowl of lukewarm, pasty oatmeal I listened to Jody, the hotel's main desk assistant manager, talk to our little group that included people from all compass points of the United States, also here for a summer of adventure.

"…So this guy comes down to complain about the noise and I'm trying to be sympathetic, but I explain a refund isn't possible after he's spent a whole night here…"

I was hearing bits and pieces, battling the fog of fatigue from two and quarter hours of sleep.

"… I understand sir, but that's part of the package when you

Chapter 13

stay in an historic lodge like this one. It's the original heating system and the pipes expand and contract with the hot water. We can't do anything about it."

Now I was awake.

"That was the heating system that kept me up last night?" I blurted out. "Does that go on *every* night?"

Jody gave me the pitying look reserved for the uninitiated. "Until summer arrives." She turned her attention back to her main audience.

"The guy's making a scene and people are waiting, so I say 'Sir, refunding in this case isn't our policy. I'm sorry but I have to take care of these other customers now.'"

In the land of extended winters, June in the Rockies can be notoriously cold and wet, and it was only the sixth of the month. I then recalled how my boss had called me at home recently and, with a tone in his voice that implied thanks were due, said he'd found me a room in the Chalet, the quietest dorm at East Glacier.

My wife Susan's summer job was in retail, working the camp store at Two Medicine, about twenty minutes away and one of the prettiest commutes in the world. Her job started in May, so she had a three-week jump on me learning the ropes. She'd already settled into a room in the 'mature' women's dorm (they called it Menopause Manor, cute). She liked it there but was willing to relocate if there was a quieter dorm for me. So, on my second day, Human Resources Department found an apartment for us in Girl's Dorm Number One.

Our new room had its own Lilliputian bathroom with shower and toilet, but no space for a sink which was found in the main room. Apparently, we were lucky because only returning employees usually got such a palace. Almost everyone else walked down the hall to a common bathroom. Workmen brought in a huge, standup dressing closet, and with a table, a couple of chairs, and an old lumpy queen bed there was little room left to walk around. The carpet was thin, the color an indeterminate smudgy brown. It looked like it had never been replaced. Susan personalized the place with some things from her old room and we settled in, hoping it would work out, but with a lump of doubt lodged somewhere in our collective solar plexus.

For the first day or two, the idea of living in a girl's dorm had sounded appealing, in a sophomoric sort of way. Here, there were girls from nearby Kalispell, girls from out of state, girls from Canada, New Zealand, Australia, and especially girls from Eastern Europe, countries like Bulgaria, Czechoslovakia, Romania, Poland, and Hungary. Memories of living in de facto coed dorms at college pleasantly swirled around my brain.

Reality soon caught up with fantasy. We were the old folks in this place by twenty-five or thirty years and one forgets just how much energy the young have for extended partying. Many of these girls were away from home for the first time and they meant to make the most of it. Truthfully, I didn't care that the place was dreary, furniture was chipped and scratched, the shower curtain was mildewed, that the toilet ran incessantly, or even that I sometimes slept on the floor because the bed sagged in the middle and was too narrow for two. After several nights of poor sleep, all I really cared about was that the place should be *quiet* after ten o'clock, as posted.

A week had passed, it was 2 AM, and flashbacks of reading *The Gulag Archipelago* came to mind, specifically Solzhenitsyn's descriptions of torture in prison. How they sat you in a cubicle with the glare of a bare, electric light bulb on the ceiling day and night. And how a guard would come by every fifteen minutes to make sure you were awake (they never let you nod off). It only takes a few days of sleep and dream deprivation to drive a person insane. A prisoner would say anything just to get some sleep, and guards had their confession to justify you rotting in a Siberian jail cell.

Chapter 13

Of course, my analogy is over-the-top, but those were my thoughts as I lay next to my softly breathing wife as the next wave of girls, just off their restaurant shift, blew through like a herd of plains bison that once roamed these parts. The boys were not far off. Even though the party was at the end of the hundred-yard-long building, all the laughter and shouting could be heard in our room despite a humidifier going for white noise, wearing the best earplugs available, and a pillow crammed over the upside ear. As the cacophony reached its peak, my wife woke with a groan.

"Godammit," she said, for maybe the third time in a decade and a half. This time I got up and called Security on the house phone. Susan watched with the door slightly ajar as the night guards filed the revelers out, accompanied by a stray mongrel dog. Suddenly, one of the inebriated young men poked his head into our room, startling Susan backward and made a rude remark. It was 3 AM by the time all was quiet. My driver training period had ended the day before and the following day was to be my first official time driving the Red Bus.

To be a Jammer, we were told, is something of an honor. It's a summer tradition that goes back to 1913, soon after the park was formed. Typically, the drivers were college men from Ivy League schools on summer vacation. Back then they had to obey strict rules of conduct and dress. On the other hand, they got lots of attention from many young and not so young ladies. The name Jammer came about when drivers were heard grinding gears on the buses' unsynchronized manual transmissions while climbing steep grades. In 2004, with fairer hiring practices, we saw women, minorities, and retired folks in the driver's seat.

The first generation of tour buses in the Park were primitive and broke down on a regular basis. Roads were unpaved. In the monsoon-like summer of 1915, crews were stationed at trouble spots to rescue vehicles mired in mud. In the mid-1930s the White Motor Corporation built five hundred, state-of-the-art tour buses destined for many national parks of the West. They were long and wide, beautifully designed to the last detail, with leather seats, solid oak doors, and roll-back canvas tops. It was a treat just to see them on the highway, and to ride in one was to be royalty for a day. Generations of Glacier visitors have fallen in love with them. The service was extended to other parks like Yosemite, but only in Yellowstone and Glacier has the tradition survived.

Red Bus number 102, Glacier National Park

In 1991, transmissions were upgraded from manual to automatic. A strut taken out to accommodate the new transmission put stress on the frame and cracks began to appear. The Red Buses were deemed unsafe to drive in 1991 and taken off the roads with no plans for their return. An outpouring of dismay from residents in nearby Kalispell and around the country

Chapter 13

convinced GPI to find a solution. Finally, Ford Motor Company stepped up to the plate: the buses were shipped back to Michigan by train; Ford lifted the bodies off the undercarriages; brand new chassis' and transmissions were built and the original bodies repositioned. The replacement engine was a Ford 327 V8 bi-fuel, burning propane and gasoline. The cost came to about a quarter of a million dollars apiece. Thirty-three buses numbered 79 through 99 and 101 to112, returned triumphantly to Glacier in 2001. Number 78 has never been operated and is slated to reside in the Smithsonian in Washington D.C. Number 100 remains in its original livery and is used as a static model at East Glacier. Today, more popular than ever, GPI's Red Buses are one of the longest, continuously operated transport services in the United States.

Susan took a snapshot of me in my official Jammer duds against the apartment's faded and peeled once-white walls. Except for the starched white shirt, everything was brown, including the tie, jacket with GPI logo, comfortable slacks, belt, and hiking boots. Even the baseball cap was brown with the GPI logo in front. I affixed my nametag to the back of it so riders could see it. It displayed my first name and my state, like this:

Ken
California

As time in Glacier passed, I'd forget it was there and vaguely wonder why strangers called me by name.

At 8:15 AM at the transportation shack (HQ), I was sweeping cracker and cookie crumbs and empty paper wrappers off the floor of my assigned bus, a job belonging to yesterday's driver. Yellow pollen from adjacent pine trees covered the bumpers, windows, and running boards. From the locked cabinet in the back, I found a *California duster*, an oversize brush with bristles soft as down that don't scratch the paint job. At 8:45 AM I drove the bus to the lodge and checked in with Angela at Transportation—a dead ringer for the actress Diana Rigg, although she was far too young to know that reference.

I studied the dispatch she handed me, a list of the names and total number of people signed up for the day. Hawkins, party of nineteen. That's odd, we were informed at orientation a full bus was seventeen.

"Hawkins, party of nineteen for the Circle Tour" I announced self-consciously. No response. Other drivers were gathering their brood and heading out on time. Nineteen people and none were present. I puzzled over the dispatch again when suddenly Mike was there, the boss's assistant.

"There's little kids in this group," he explained. "Some will sit on the adults' laps."

I looked at him quizzically.

"See, the thing is, this tour's a charter, not a regular run."

This new information was of little help since I had nothing to compare it to.

The party slowly dribbled in during the next hour, during which I was asked if an open container of hot chocolate was okay to bring and where could two coolers of food and drink be put, neither of which were allowed. With much effort and struggle, the two coolers were placed on the floor in the narrow back row where the kids wouldn't mind using them as footrests. Finally, an hour late, we were ready to pull out when two Jack Russell terriers showed up, one directly behind me, one on the lap of Pete, the doyen of the group, riding shotgun. Nothing was said at orientation about dogs, although we were warned we'd have to think on our feet. I asked Larry, a veteran driver getting ready for the Great Northern Tour at 10 AM. He'd never encountered the issue in seven years. Mike had gone and the boss, who booked this tour, was conspicuously absent. We departed.

Two months earlier I had been sent a manual for drivers in an e-mail attachment. Back then in the early 2000s, it took two disks to download. At 300 printed pages it covered every aspect

Chapter 13

of the park's cultural and natural history and I'd been studying it religiously. By the time you had finished it you knew more than most park rangers. But Red Bus drivers didn't have a set script to follow, like many tour guides nowadays, and while it kept things fresh for you and your riders, it was scary the first time. Horror stories circulated from veteran drivers about their first day, one young man stumbling over his narrative, nervous and sweating, fabricating stories for questions he couldn't answer, and finally giving up on speaking altogether.

My role as tour leader would be severely challenged on that first outing. Six kids from three to eleven years old were already creating bedlam, and a couple of adults were helping them. We had eight hours to go on 140 miles of highway, a third of that time on the spectacular Going-To-The-Sun road, so narrow and precipitous that many tourists distrust their own driving ability (that's why they're on the bus). The Hawkins party had no idea this was my first day.

I tried to impart some knowledge as we headed up Highway 2.

"See that beaver dam along the river? Beaver were sacred to the Blackfeet Indians. They refused the Hudson Bay Company's offer of money for pelts. It was the beaver that transformed a raw, bare, glacially carved landscape by slowing the river's flow, filling in the boulder fields with soil, allowing forest to take hold, bringing in the moose, the waterfowl, the predators, a whole freaking ecosystem. The beaver started all that."

A cold rain beat against the ground and the bus's heating system didn't reach past the second row. At Marias Pass, marking the Continental Divide, nobody was even thinking about getting out to view the bronze, oversize statue of John Franklin Stevens, the first surveyor of the pass and later the chief engineer of the Panama Canal. A fifty-foot replica of the Washington Monument placed to commemorate Teddy Roosevelt's conservation work didn't tempt them either. As we pulled onto the deserted highway, some wag in the back joked, "It's going to be a long trip eh, Ken?"

Lunchtime. The group were supposed to picnic on the shores of Lake McDonald. I was looking forward to an hour with other drivers at Lake McDonald EDR.

"Ken, join us for lunch?" invited Pete.

Caught off guard, I stuttered an acceptance. The meal turned out to be delicious, gourmet even. Fresh albacore caught off the California coast with potato salad and other temptations. I started to relax. The rain had stopped, and the sun was trying to poke through. I could even ignore the Jack Russell terriers as they terrorized the campground.

"Wanda, get back here, *Wanda!*" The other one was named Wilma. With their white, bristly fur, dogged determined expressions, and chin stubble they looked like little mountain goats.

After lunch, it was photo-op time. With five cameras strung around my neck, I photographed the Hawkins party in various groupings, draped around the Red Bus like it was a movie star. Kids hung from the struts of the rearview mirrors.

With the help of a more able passenger, we rolled the canvas top back on the bus, making sure the stretch cords were tight around the side hooks. The bus was built just for this—unobstructed views of the most awesome highway in America. It was back in 1912 that William Logan (for whom Logan Pass was named) first envisioned a motor road crossing the heart of the park so everyone, young and old, firm and infirm, could see this national treasure. Surveying was completed just before the winter of 1924 and work began the following spring. Coming together from east and west like the transcontinental railroad, it was completed in 1932 at the cost of 2.5 million dollars and three lives. Each spring, snow clearing must begin in April to finish the job by June, sometimes through drifts fifty feet high.

Now we were *en regalia*. Majestically, we motored at 33 miles per hour (optimum speed according to the driver's manual)

Chapter 13

through the easternmost temperate rain forest in the United States, full of dense cedar, hemlock, and the bright, lime-green foliage of larch.

"Off to your right ladies and gentlemen, avalanche chutes like alpine bowling alleys scour the four thousand-foot cliffs of Mt. Cannon. Did you know avalanches are the number-one killer of mountain goats? In the spring ravenous grizzlies will sniff around the base of the slides, looking for a meal of fresh frozen goat."

At the west tunnel, I played a joke learned from a more experienced driver. With no cars behind us, we slowed to a crawl through the tunnel so they could get a framed photo of snow-covered Heavens Peak through the 'window'.

"Okay everyone, look up and right just as we leave the tunnel because an eagle's nest is about a hundred feet above." All expectantly looked up as an early-season waterfall splashed their faces with droplets.

The previous summer the park had been shut down by wildfires for a month, leaving many drivers at loose ends. At the Loop, where the highway swings from due west to due east, the fire suddenly raged out of control, racing upslope nearly to Granite Park Chalet, three thousand feet above the canyon. Here at the Loop, you could still see the melted remnants of the plastic outhouses, glistening in the sun like candle wax.

Farther up the road at Haystack Falls, raging creek waters passed unimpeded under a beautifully designed bridge. It's one example of how the road engineers succeeded in integrating the road without compromising the scenery. We stopped for a breath of crisp air and a stint of leg stretching. The whole world was alive with tumbling waterfalls, and snow graced the high peaks, the highest of which held wind-plastered rime.

One of the adults asked if the water tumbling down the steep hillside was safe to drink.

"We can't really recommend it. A nasty bug called giardia is pretty common in the Rockies."

"But it's probably okay, right?"

I could see he was determined and just shrugged. I was only a glorified chauffeur that day. Far above was the heavily traveled Highline Trail, popular with people and plenty of mountain goats too. The goats used the trail like other hikers, passing the very stream in question.

The curious passenger walked over with a canteen, filled it, and drank.

"That's the best tasting water I've ever had," he shouted from across the road.

Meanwhile, in the back of the bus, a man popped open a soda can from the cooler, which, due to the elevation change, promptly went off like a fireworks sparkler. The sticky contents spilled over onto the leather seats, seat backing, and floor. His wife, bless her, took the responsibility of mopping up the mess.

"Wanda, *Wanda*, get *back* here!" The feistiest of the Jack Russell terriers had escaped. She was off the leash and on a run down the steep, rocky hillside, looking like she'd got a bead on Lake McDonald, two thousand vertical feet below.

"*Wanda*, come back here *now*!" Pete bellowed. The whole crew was now gathered on the cliff edge to see the drama. I doubt the Rangers would look the other way if she injured or killed any wildlife. I scanned the highway for the white, green-striped cruisers that might spell trouble. Wanda, who'd been uncontrollable, spending more time on the dashboard than Pete's lap, and obstructing my side-view mirror, had found a way to expend some of that irrepressible energy. Finally, she made her way upslope again but a hundred yards further up the highway, where she jumped into the arms of a stranger. With much admonishment, the leash was secured to her collar and the other end tied to the bus's seat bar. With no visible sign of shame, Wanda stuck her mug out the window with a self-satisfied air of an adventure well executed.

Chapter 13

"Ken, let's get a picture of you two."

I put my best professional face forward, sharing the space with a mutt who looked for all the world like a miniature tough, old Scottish mountain goat.

This summer and for several more, the Jammers had an added challenge due to long-overdue road work. At the concrete Jersey barriers, the road turned into one lane. It was signaled, the wait a full five minutes. I got pulled up short by the red light, first in line. The over-wide, twenty-five-foot-long Red Bus had inches to spare between the rock wall and the barriers, which sat on the edge of a thousand-foot drop. Here you had to watch your side mirrors constantly.

"Pete, I'm not moving until Wanda is constrained." Pete hadn't heard that tone in my voice before.

Suddenly, without warning or permission and with a nimbleness belying his ample girth, Pete stepped out the door, placing Wanda on the front seat, and walked in front of the bus for a picture. The light turned green. A dozen cars were behind me and by the time Pete returned the light was red again. For the second time, we waited for the five-minute cycle to complete. The reputation of the Red Bus was such that no honking of horns or angry voices were heard behind us. Maybe they thought we had a perfectly valid reason to miss the signal.

Negotiating the Jersey Barriers perfectly as we practiced so many times, I was suddenly feeling free. Let the group do whatever they want. I told them an apocryphal-sounding story one veteran swore was true, about a driver who took one hand off the wheel and pointed out Bird Woman Falls, a spectacular, 400-foot freefalling curtain of water across the canyon.

"Driver," said a nervous passenger, "please use both hands."

"Yes ma'am," said the obliging jammer, and repeated his line, taking both hands off the wheel to gesture at the falls.

The group's main objective was to see wildlife. Nearing Logan Pass we slowed to a stop. A large and noble mountain goat (they weigh up to 300 pounds) stood in the middle of the roadway eyeing the traffic he'd stopped. There he was, a true symbol of Glacier Park, emblazoned as a logo on Visitor Center knickknacks, sweatshirts, and many official documents, including my own paltry paycheck. Slowly and regally, he moved to the side and nimbly leaped on top of a low stone barrier wall, stopped and peered into the Red Bus itself as if looking for a spare seat. Cameras were clicking spasmodically now, full-frame shots without a zoom. Seeing that no room existed in the overcrowded transport, he dropped to the other side and blandly continued to graze, unaware that he had just made everyone's day.

"Did you guys know that goats are attracted to the taste of radiator coolant? ... Yeah, it doesn't harm them at all, but it keeps them from freezing in the harsh winters."

Logan Pass presented a 360-degree panorama of snowy, Matterhorn-like peaks atop the Continental Divide—Oberlin, Reynolds, Bear Hat, Clements, Heavy Runner, Matahtopa, Red Chief, Going to the Sun, Piegan, Pollack, and beyond Bishops' Cap and the Garden Wall. All draped in snowy mantles. The bus slid into one of the specially designated long lanes next to other buses.

"Twenty minutes folks," I said, knowing it would be thirty.

The boardwalk to Hidden Lake overlook was closed due to snow, but the kids didn't care. They came back cold and wet with their pants soaked from sliding sled-like down the banks next to the Visitor Center. Then, it was second gear all the way down the east side of the Divide, the group quiet enough for a glaciology lesson at Jackson Glacier overlook. At the current attrition rate, the icy fastnesses that gives the park its name will be gone by 2030. Whether you call it part of a natural cycle or blame it on our global experiment with fossil fuels, you better get there soon if you haven't seen it. In 1910, the year the park was established, there were 150 glaciers. In 2004, at the time of

Chapter 13

this trip, there were 27. And at the time of writing, only 25.

Our last stop was Sunrift Gorge, an arrow-straight, slot canyon fed all summer by a sluice of numb-cold ice water off the Sexton Glacier. Sweat trickled down my face and tickled my armpits under a sun now beaming out of a cloudless sky. The long underwear under this uniform, my savior this morning, was now my tormentor.

Later, we cruised beautiful ten-mile-long St. Mary Lake, ruffled ice blue waters punctuated only by the Hershey's Kiss of Wild Goose Island. To our left, the vast meadows of Two Dog Flat wouldn't have elk herds until the fall mating season.

"BEAR!" I blurted out as a black shape disappeared into the shadows of the shoreline cottonwoods, too fast for most to see. They were disappointed when there was no safe place to pull over. As we left the park at St. Mary Visitor Center, I waved to the kiosk ranger and punched the accelerator for the long climb on Highway 89.

Wildlife sightings are common on the east side highway. My party and I saw horses and cattle belonging to the Blackfeet Nation. Later in the year, within a ten-minute span, my wife and I saw a bear cub cross the road, two moose cows on the side of the road, and a full-grown bull moose with a massive rack twice as high as our little Subaru cross the road and disappear into the brush with that majestic and comic gait.

"Don't hit any cattle," we were warned by the boss, "because it will be a prize animal you've hit, and it'll cost you out of pocket." A figure of four or five thousand dollars was thrown about, enough to erase a summer's earnings. Only later did I realize the boss was probably blowing hot air, worried about GPI's insurance costs.

The final hill before East Glacier looked over a vast, fenced meadow on both sides of the two-lane blacktop, with horses of the Blackfeet-owned concession grazing in the belly-deep grass after a day's work. Parts of the meadow were still submerged and wouldn't dry up until August. We passed East Glacier's golf course, which sported frequent grizzly sightings on the ninth hole and begged the question, can a golf cart outrun a Griz? (Not a chance, better carry your pepper spray.) After turning into the main entrance to the Lodge, we passed a cute brown cottage with bright red trim and gorgeous displays of red flowers in oversize clay flowerpots flanking the walkway.

"That's Mr. Tibbet's place, our postmaster," I said, anticipating questions as per the manual. "This is his fifty-fourth summer in a row at Glacier Park."

Up the final hill with a flourish to the Lodge entrance.

"Thanks everyone for surviving with me on my *very first* Red Bus tour."

Handshakes all around, final goodbyes, one man invited me to drop by his business in the Sierra foothills next fall. Pete pulled a bill out of his pocket and handed it to me. I thanked him and put it in my pocket without looking.

"Is this really your first tour?"

Passenger-less, I ducked under the railroad overpass to the Exxon for propane. Back at headquarters, it was time to clean up. Wash down the bus. Sweep out the floors. Collect a small hill of soda cans, beer bottles, potato chip bags, candy wrappers. Sweep out the sandwich leftovers and the pretzel crumbs onto the ground.

Statia, who had been accepted as a trainee late in the month, walked up. She was returning from her first tour also.

"How'd it go?"

"Oh, pretty wild." Then I remembered and reached into my pocket to pull out the crumpled bill, curious for the first time. I had trouble focusing at first—it was the world-weary countenance of Ben Franklin staring back at me.

The temporary lift that tour gave me was short-lived. Back at Girl's Dorm Number One, the honeymoon was long over. Most girls worked at the East Glacier Lodge restaurant, a place

Chapter 13

with a dour reputation. Shifts at Glacier ran 24/7 so I was awakened most nights by loud, drunken voices, heavy footsteps, and slamming of wooden doors with their metal locks echoing and reverberating through the thin, un-insulated plywood walls. I averaged four hours of sleep a night. Every morning I dreaded looking at the dispatch sheet. Toward the end of June, I was assigned to eight days of work in a row. The last four days included three circle tours on Going-to-the-Sun Road (GTTS) and a run to Waterton, Glacier's sister park in Canada. Effectively these were ten- to twelve-hour days, though you were docked about two hours for meals. The main tourist season, which runs from the Fourth of July to the middle of August, was looming. Every day I managed to drag myself to work on time, wondering if somewhere on the road my cumulative fatigue would lead to inattention, a wreck, an injury, or worse. My emotional state was eggshell-fragile and a breakdown of some sort seemed inevitable.

After some difficult soul searching, I gave my notice at the end of the month and launched Plan B. For the next six weeks I stayed at walk-in campgrounds at Two Medicine, St. Mary, Rising Sun, and Cut Bank for three bucks a night and made hiking the park my day job. Knowing I'd be hiking alone most of the time, I bought the forty-dollar insurance plan—Counter Assault pepper spray with its own holster belt and Velcro security strap.

And that's when I entered a state of grace. Immediately I began to sleep full nights. I shared the park with mountain goats (many), mountain sheep (a group of seven at Triple Divide Pass), grouse (two families), water ouzels (fifteen sightings), black bear (lots), grizzlies (six in one day) and, most impressive of all, the bull moose. Each day I came back satisfied there was no better way to spend my time. I walked from five to twenty miles a day in Glacier's alpine Garden of Eden. The aches and pains I thought were permanent virtually disappeared.

Often, I saw my former colleagues driving the Red Bus or the white van shuttles and frequently they waived the fee for me. They weren't getting the time off as promised. They were overworked and some were feeling harried, frustrated.

"Five or six days on, two days off a week, sometimes staggered," had been the promise from the boss back in February. Two days off a month was closer to the truth. Over-booked and under-staffed was looking like the true company policy.

One day when Susan and I completed the Highline Trail from Logan Pass to the Loop, we were picked up in the shuttle by a sweet young woman named Rachel who had roomed across from us during training before being stationed at Many Glacier. She admitted to working her 24th day in a row. Toward the middle of August, another woman confessed to working 50 hours of *overtime* that week. There were those who needed the money and those who didn't, and some of those stayed out of loyalty anyway.

And there were many who loved the job no matter what. One of them was Jammer Joe, a retired pig farmer from Iowa, one of the gentlest, kindest, funniest, and most considerate human beings I've ever met. He'd raised four kids, worked his tail off all his life, and was just glad to have someone else call the shots for a while. His must have been one of three or four families in America that wasn't dysfunctional. Every time a driver was sick, on leave, or too tired to work, Joe was ready to step in. No complaining, no whining, just some fine-tuning on the attitude adjustment and he was good to go. He liked to quote a sign posted at the GPI transportation shack—"Blessed are those who are flexible, for they shall not be bent out of shape." Oh man, did I try to live up to that. But I suspect it was meant more for labor than for management.

For me, the decision to leave was the right one. I had hoped to integrate work and play that summer and ended up working then playing. I have fond memories of both.

CHAPTER 13

Old Man Lake and Mt. Flinsch, Glacier National Park

Chapter 14
Pigeon Spire Solo

We need adventure. It's in our blood. It will not go away. The mountains will continue to call because they uniquely fulfill our need for communion with nature, as well as our hunger for adventure.
—Royal Robbins

After the Glacier park gig ended, part of my summer of 2004 was spent in neighboring Canada. I was 53 at the time of this ascent. It would prove to be one of the last notable outings in my mountaineering career. Age and circumstances brought on a change in lifestyle and, like my hero Royal Robbins, I found new excitement and challenges in whitewater kayaking. I look back on Pigeon Spire with fondness and nostalgia.

Canadians like their gravel roads smooth. The 45 kilometers (28 miles) from Brisco to Bugaboo Provincial Park in southern British Columbia, was in great shape and any low-slung car, like the rental I was driving, can cruise it at a decent clip. The first view of the Bugaboos is overwhelming. A massive granite spire called the Houndstooth, thousands of feet above, thrusts its way out of the lower Bugaboo Glacier, surrounded by a fearsome-looking, chaotic icefield of hundreds of crevasses and seracs. You pass the lodge that caters to rich tourists who come for heli-skiing, then reach the road's end. Here, the gravel parking lot had not changed since my last visit, with the trailhead to Kain Hut and the Bugaboos nearby. And just like before, every car was surrounded by a makeshift barrier of chicken wire propped up by sticks and stones and whatever else could be scavenged. Porcupines were the cause of this unusual sight. It seemed a potassium/sodium imbalance in their diet made them crave salt from any source and the resulting damage could be your brake lines, even tires. I noted the only thing that had changed was the absence of the little wooden shack that held the chicken wire, but plenty lay around.

My threadbare climbing pack, the Arcteryx Bora 40, was designed for day use, not backpacking, but there was no other choice—when I left home in June for a summer in Glacier Park, alpine climbing was not on the itinerary. I could make two trips to the hut and back, but the idea was unappealing. A frustrating hour and a half ended with 60 pounds of climbing gear, food, sleeping bag, clothes, and extraneous necessities stuffed into the sagging, misshapen rucksack. The rope and Thermarest were tied to the sides while my climbing shoes, down vest, stove and helmet dangled from carabiners at all angles, making the whole affair look like a cartoon caricature of a bum's home on his back. A quarter mile-down the trail I was second-guessing myself.

As a distraction from this suffering, the memory of another trip came back fresh to my mind. Ten years previously we'd hired a horse packer to carry our gear 17 miles into Lonesome Lake in the Wind Rivers of Wyoming. Robin and I had climbed Pingora, a wonderful thousand-foot tower of granite. Too much food had been brought and too little thought had gone into how much the packs would weigh on the return. Mine came to 75 pounds, fully half my body weight. My four-year-old climbing rope was in decent shape but nevertheless went front and center on the chopping block. Just before I abandoned it on a rock, a National Outdoor Leadership School instructor came by with a group of novices and he was happy to have it.

But this day I needed everything my poor back was supporting. The initial pleasant stroll turned to steep, loose trail, slab scrambling, steps protected by railings, and even ladder-

Chapter 14

climbing over vertical rock steps. In only 2 miles the trail climbed over 2,000 feet. It was 85° F out according to two brothers who were headed back for a second carry to ensure their beer cache was adequate.

Nearing the hut there was a high stream crossing facilitated by a narrow wooden board with no railings. I'd never heard of anyone losing their balance here, but a fall wouldn't be pretty. The Kain Hut is a magnificent three-story backcountry lodge, anchored to solid granite overlooking the Bugaboo Glacier. Its prominent teal roof can easily be seen from the summit of Bugaboo Spire. Built in 1972, it houses 40 people in a dormitory style, sports a modern kitchen, is heated by wood stove, and provides a great social space for mountaineers. Beware though if you wish to sleep past 3 AM — though the posted regulations state no sorting of gear in the wee hours, rules are often broken. Towering above the hut is Snowpatch Spire with its signature snowfield, one of the possible objectives of this trip, if I could find a partner.

I was greeted by Felix the hut keeper and inquired straightaway about partners. He didn't know of anyone but recommended posting a notice. He directed me to Boulder Camp a fair way below. The sites were small and perched among huge boulders just above the colossal 2,000 drop I'd come up. I got a quick sponge bath, cooked a meal, talked to Carston and Darcy, the two brothers who had returned with more beer, took two Alleve, and passed out for the night...

The following day was spent pleasantly at the empty camp lounging in my Thermarester, reading Dostoevsky's *Crime and Punishment*. A quick stroll down to the stone outhouse revealed the true gem of the camp, featuring a picture-window view of Houndstooth, and the lower Bugaboo Glacier. Feeling a sudden surge of energy, I bounded up the trail to post a 'partner wanted' sign, then continued up to Applebee Camp, situated on a dome of rock with stupendous views of Snowpatch and Bugaboo

Spires. Here I found everyone was disappointingly partnered up.

My expectations were along the lines of the American Alpine Club camp in the Tetons where I found Don, a climber from the east coast, in the first five minutes of my arrival. Soon after I proposed climbing the Exum route on the Grand Teton, he spent an hour on the phone postponing his flight and other appointments. I had no such luck here. I met two young guys who gave me the beta on Pigeon Spire, commonly done solo by confident climbers. It looked like my dreams of Snowpatch were melting away.

Returning to the hut, I nearly convinced Felix we could be back from Pigeon Spire in half a day, but his responsibilities to the hut won out. I decided to solo Pigeon Spire on the morrow.

At Boulder Camp, Carston and Darcy had abandoned their latest climbing plans and having drunk all the beer were going down in the morning. They told me a story of climbing Greenland's Mt. Asgard that required two, 30-kilometer (almost 19 miles) carries of gear to the base (I wonder how much of that was beer?) Their moderate route took over 24 hours of non-stop effort. As they prepared to leave, two young speed climbers showed up, Jason Singer and Cedar Wright, who later did the same route in 3 ½ hours wearing tennis shoes. Jason had been on the ill-starred epic adventure in Kyrgyzstan when Islamic terrorists took them captive, the gripping story recounted by Greg Child in his book *Over the Edge*.

I woke at 4 AM before my watch alarm went off. Outside it was cloudy and thundershowers were predicted. My pack was down to twenty-five pounds, which included a 9mm rope, slings, a few camming devices and quickdraws, lunch, water, and a pair of new climbing shoes bought in Kalispell.

At the hut, I posted a notice of my solo attempt at Felix's request. From that point, I was on my own. Taking in the frosty mountain air, I got that distinct, edgy feeling one gets on a

Chapter 14

special adventure, one of delight and expectation tempered by a touch of anxiety. The sky was full of dark clouds with hopeful gaps between them. With the imposing Bugaboo Spire in full view, I recalled the 1991 ascent of the North East ridge with my partner Robin. Twelve parties had been on the classic route that day, but we had managed to get out in front with our greater experience on rock and a willingness to simulclimb several pitches. Late in the day, the snow-and-ice-experienced Canadians had flown by us on the descent. In fact, while we delicately approached and stepped over the final crevasse, one party literally glissaded over it like a bobsled run.

I veered off the trail before Applebee onto the glacier and headed toward the col between Snowpatch and Bugaboo Spires. It's a steep, short climb that was fanned that day by a cool morning wind. On top, I donned hat and gloves while admiring Pigeon Spire bookmarking the end of the flat Vowell Glacier. No one was around and the Bugaboos seemed to be all mine. Off to my right was the legendary Kain Route on Bugaboo Spire, done in 1916.

The crux of that route is the so-called 'gendarme', an imposing pinnacle of rock led by Kain without the benefit of pitons. It was one of the hardest routes in the Canadian Rockies at that time, described by Kain as the most difficult of his career. And what a career he had. The Austrian-born climber made over 60 first ascents in the Rockies including the seldom done Mt. Louis and the iconic Mt. Robson. Kain did all his ascents with clients, not other professionals. As he led his clients to the top of Robson, he famously told them, "Gentlemen, that is as far as I can take you." His reputation and stature have only increased over the years. A one-act play and a song have been written about his life.

Striding out across the glacier, my steps made a disturbing *whump, whump* sound, as if the snow was hollow underneath. I veered away only to find an open crevasse. Returning to the well-trodden track, I held my ice axe out in front of me in case I plunged into a crevasse. The snow softened as the glacier steepened, then at its end I clambered to the base of Pigeon. I had the place all to myself. The Howell Mountains beyond were wilder looking than anything yet, with the bergshrund a massive horizontal gash between main wall and lower snowfield. Here I took a few moments to regroup, tied on the rope backpack-style, and laced up the rock shoes. I left the helmet (no chance of rockfall on a traverse) but mistakenly chose to leave my camera. The West Ridge of Pigeon is a series of three gently rising traverses, punctuated by two dips in between. The difficulty is easy fifth class but you're not here for a technical workout. You're here for the location and the exposure.

And exposure I got in spades. The first step was straightforward and went quickly. After a quick downclimb to the first notch, I tackled the second step, a knife-edge that drops off on both sides for a thousand feet. An unroped fall would likely be fatal, a fact I was well aware of, but my confidence was high and I hummed a little tune to match my mood. Some climbers scoot across the knife-edge on their butts, but I used a low-angle layback technique, hands on the ridgeline, feet frictioning on the superb rough granite. It was an absolute joy to be here alone, surrounded by a wilderness of rock and ice and no one within sight or sound.

A hand crack appeared as the rock angle increased, but the rope remained tied to my back. At the top of the second step, I missed the easy descent to the second notch and instead downclimbed a steep section, probably harder than anything on the regular route. Now the route moved off the ridgeline to the left and suddenly the exposure went from stimulating to daunting. I stopped perplexed for several minutes, presented with a ledge of melting ice and snow. To my left, a 60–70-degree snowfield ended a few hundred feet down in a sheer cliff that dropped hundreds of feet to the Vowell Glacier.

I played it safe and uncoiled the rope, looped one end over a

Chapter 14

good horn of rock, tied the rope into my harness, tied a thin diameter perlon loop with a prussic knot from the harness to the rope, and stepped out. At that moment my eyeglasses decided to detach from my face and fell into a narrow crevice. Kneeling in the snow, I gingerly reached down a full arm's length up to my shoulder and managed to retrieve them. Continuing, I placed one or two cams in the rock wall to my right. In case of a fall, I knew from experience the prussic knot self-belay method was not infallible, but it was all I had. All went well and I placed an anchor at the far end, partially reversed my steps to remove the gear, then gave the rope a flip which obediently came off the horn.

Beyond the snowy ledge, the climbing eased and soon I was atop Pigeon Spire, surely one of the finest moderate fifth class climbs in North America. A 360-degree panorama of granite spires and snow stretched to all horizons. No wonder the Canadian Rockies are called the American Alps. Predicted thundershowers had not materialized and the sky was clear. I now worried about softening snowfields and made preparations to leave.

The rappel off the summit did not, as I hoped, take me past the snowy ledge traverse and I had to repeat all my self-belay maneuvers. From there on, the descent was nearly as enjoyable as the ascent. I took great pleasure in placing feet and hands precisely on their holds, resolving any doubt of danger. I returned to the base after a three-hour round trip, repacked, and quickly descended toward Bugaboo Spire. Midway across the glacier, I met Dave and Stoney from Applebee Camp. They had already climbed the North East ridge on Bugaboo, dropped their gear at the base, and were hustling over to Pigeon to do a tandem solo ascent.

Such energy! They seem unconcerned about crevasse danger and I wondered if my concerns were overblown. Nevertheless, I continued with caution until my return to Kain Hut by 2 PM, satisfied with one of the more beautiful alpine days of my life.

Pigeon Spire in clearing storm light

Chapter 15
The Trinity and Mr. B

We may be floating on Tao, but there is nothing wrong with steering. If Tao is like a river, it is certainly good to know where the rocks are.
—Deng Ming-Dao, Everyday Tao: Living with Balance and Harmony

"Oh Eeyore you are wet!" said Piglet, feeling him. Eeyore shook himself, and asked somebody to explain to Piglet what happened when you had been inside a river for quite a long time.
—AA Milne, Winnie the Pooh

Dark green forests yielded an electric, sky blue ribbon of water, foaming white now and then as it passed over submerged rocks. The Trinity! I was so excited I wanted to go boating right then, but evening was upon us. Kaley and his grandson Christian arrived at East Fork Campground only minutes behind Harrison, Julie and I. Kaley had driven a crazy zig-zag course from Truckee that required crossing the State once and the Coast Range twice in order to pick up his grandson in the Trinity county river town of Dinsmore. Our fern-filled, fir-canopied canyon with a tumbling icy creek nearby was like something out of Canada, not northern California.

The following day, we would paddle.

The Trinity is the Klamath's largest tributary, flowing 165 miles from the Scott Mountains to its confluence with the Klamath at Weitchpec, part of the Yurok Indian nation. Despite four years of drought, that summer of 2016 clear and beautiful water flowed from Clair Engel Lake at around 700 cubic feet per second. It was easily enough water to float not only the ten-foot inflatable kayaks Julie and I brought, but also Harrison's fourteen-foot raft he was sharing with Kaley and Christian. Where the water pooled in the calm stretches, the river was transparent to twenty feet, and we could see steelhead trout at the bottom.

I was hanging back from the group, delirious with the simple pleasure of movement over water. Here, I was not only captain of my boat, but captain of my life. Decisions mattered. An idyllic day could turn ugly, if, for example, I ran into that grove of willow trees coming up on river right, bobbing innocently in the current. These are known as strainers. They allow water through but hold back larger objects, just like a kitchen colander would do. First, you are caught in the branches, then, pushed down by the force of the water.

But right then, I didn't have a single worry on my mind. My kayak was moving in sync with the current, responsive, and alive. Past the strainer, I hunkered down in my seat, letting the brilliance of the sun bathe my face. Treetops and grey granite cliffs floated by, reminding me of childhood rides in the back of the station wagon. As I paid close attention to the details around me, time slowed down. There was nowhere else I wanted to be—it was the best of all places.

On a whim, I grabbed my paddle and rowed hard to sneak up on the raft. But Harrison, on the stern with guide paddle in hand, turned around before I could launch my ambush. I was outnumbered three to one, but all four of us got equally soaked after some furious splashing. The river is a great place to be when the summer heat is on.

We could hear the rapid before it was visible. It was time to get serious. Canyon walls narrowed as I got that flutter of anticipation in the gut, a mix of fear and excitement. White, caboose-size boulders appeared, spread like giant chessboard pieces.

Chapter 15

Julie had gone from newbie-cautious to leading the pack and Harrison was right behind her. I slowed down to prolong and enjoy the experience by turning the kayak 45 degrees to the current and back paddling. Now I wove between the chess pieces, left to right, then right to left, like a carom ball in an old pinball machine. But here the idea was not to bounce off the bumpers but gracefully slide by.

The boulders ended and suddenly the river's entire volume converged into a slot only six feet wide, churning solid white, with a shocking ledge drop of several feet. My boat and I had never done such a rapid. Suppressing excitement, I kept the bow at a diagonal to the current until the last moment, and then with a single stroke straightened it to plumb. Time and I suddenly rushed forward as the current grabbed hold and flung us through the foaming turnstile. My bow plunged steeply and the boat went vertical. For a moment it was up to the river, not me, and I disappeared beneath the waters. Re-emerging, I was still upright and gave a spontaneous shout for joy, startling my river mates just below. That's what it's all about!

We moved our base camp from East Fork Camp many miles up the highway to Hayden Flat, a strategic location to facilitate shuttles and eliminate long drives. But as soon as we pulled into the upper site (the lower was full) it was clear we had gone from Eden to Hell. Surrounding us were groves of listless, dry, and malevolent pine trees. The hot air was stagnant and suffocating. Nothing moved but malignant mosquitoes and logging trucks, their sound rising upslope, pillaging the canyon's peace. Julie and I were horrified, but the others seemed content, and another move was out-voted.

Later that night in the tent the air was stifling, intolerable. I tried sleeping outside but it was soon clear that the heat would keep the whining insects up all night. There was only one thing to do. I rolled up the pad and sleeping bag, said goodnight to Julie who had chosen to stay, and walked a quarter mile down the camp road, across the highway, then past the lower camp and down to a level sandbar that earlier was crowded with bathers. The sandbar was now deserted, not even a late-night amorous couple wrestling it out. Here the air was ten degrees cooler, the mosquitoes were gone, the nearby waterfall provided soothing white noise and I had found a way back to Eden. As I fell into a delicious sleep, I pitied the others at what I dubbed Camp Fools on the Hill. This sandbar would be my home for the remainder of the trip.

I kicked back and put my paddle aside. Hitchhikers floated on the bobbing current — green willow branches, driftwood, and the summer snow of white willow catkins. To my left a bright orange fluttering attracted Julie. Something was alive out there. She tried to scoop up the object with her paddle but drifted on without it. Curious, I headed over. It was a helpless butterfly, nearly drowned. My paddle rescue was successful and I lay him out limp on the port tube. Within half a minute he was drying out and testing his wings, one of which had suffered a semi-circular bite. He worked his wings like bellows, slowly and sensuously, his near-drowning already forgotten.

Rough water was coming up.

"Look out Mr. B!" I warned my new passenger.

I encouraged the butterfly to crawl onto my paddle and placed him inside the kayak where he wouldn't get washed away. The wave was bigger than expected, breaking over the bow, and Mr. B sloshed around in the prop wash. When the boat drained my new friend was once again soaked flat. Gamely, he picked himself up and crawled this time onto the starboard tube to dry in the summer heat. Soon he was exploring his surroundings again like nothing had happened.

Mr. B was now in front playing Bow Prince and enjoying the slight rush of cooler air coming off the river as we coasted along at three miles an hour. My river mates knew by now I had a hitchhiker.

Chapter 15

"Hey, I saw that butterfly earlier," said Harrison. "Looks like a fish wanted him for breakfast."

A dull roar meant more white water ahead.

"Mr. B, are you crazy? Get down from there!"

I was too busy to help but peripherally noticed the butterfly dashed to the bottom of the boat once again and disappearing out of sight behind me. This time I was sure he was gone for good. How could a helpless creature weighing a hundredth of an ounce survive that onslaught? After the rapid, I looked back. There he was, fluttering his one and a half wings and drying out. Mr. B seemed to be enjoying the trip. Most of us think of butterflies as some of the more fragile and delicate creatures on earth. I was starting to form another opinion.

But now an increasing roar downriver meant Big French Creek Rapid was approaching. These were some of the biggest waves of the trip. I could put Mr. B in a waterproof Pelican case along with my camera but there wasn't time. Julie was nervous about this rapid and hung back. Harrison took the lead while I told Julie to follow my line. Big frothy waves enveloped my boat. These I could take head-on no problem—it was the lateral waves that were the sneaky ones, coming without warning from left or right trying to tip me over. I braced repeatedly with the flat of my paddle either port or starboard side, like a frantic hula dancer on steroids. Then a huge sinkhole appeared on the right, ready to suck me under like food scraps into a garbage disposal. I managed to skirt that on the left and got flushed out to calmer water.

I looked back. Julie had made it through the main excitement only to get upset by an invisible, barely submerged rock. Bad luck. Over she went along with her boat. I intercepted her Tomcat before it escaped down river and stashed it in some convenient rocks. Julie, per the book, had kept her paddle, swum to shore, and escaped with only a bruise and scrape. Meanwhile, the raft had circled back via a helpful eddy to see how we were doing.

"God dang it, that was pretty fun huh?"

We took time out to recuperate. We were done with rapids for the day and the rest was a family rated class 1. Suddenly I remembered my erstwhile companion.

"Oh shit, where's Mr. B?"

I had quickly become fond of my Lepidopteran friend.

"What's that on the back of your hat?" exclaimed Kaley.

"What?!"

I loosened the cord tie under my chin and lifted off the broad brim hat that had been my sunshade for a decade. There, lightly clutching with his stick-like legs and staring me right in the eyes was Mr. B. If he had eyelashes he'd have been batting them coquettishly.

"I can't believe this."

Mr. B had survived the biggest waves on the river and made it look easy. He was enjoying this as much as we were. With a heart like his and arms instead of wings, I would have had a great second mate.

We pushed off for the final two miles. Mr. B now had only one and quarter wings left. He was also walking around drunkenly and insisted on exploring the outside edge of the port tube. He fell out. I rescued him only to repeat the sequence several more times. Once he almost went under for good. Tenderly I placed him on my hat. I could feel him crawl around on my neck and face.

A familiar sandbar appeared around the last bend and we ran the boats aground. Away from the cooling river, we walked into a wall of heat. Camp was now only a few minutes' walk away since Julie and I had convinced the group to move from Fools on the Hill to the lower river camp after the weekend crowd disappeared.

We'd all had an incredible day, for me the most memorable of the trip. Beers in hand, butts in camp chairs, we luxuriated in the afterglow of a day well spent. Mr. B was looking tired after

Chapter 15

his big adventure. Christian had the idea of feeding him some leaves but when that failed to entice him, he poured out a few drops from his soda can into a saucer. Mr. B eagerly slurped it all up and more when a second ration was doled out. He perked up a noticeably and was now content to perch on my hat. After chips and salsa and more beers, two of us went to retrieve the shuttle car and I placed Mr. B in Christian's care.

"Hey, is Mr. B still there?" I asked upon our return.

I placed him on my hat again. Then something unusual happened. I could feel Mr. B crawl onto my shoulder, then down my arm and into my hand. I brought my palm level with my eyes. Mr. B's two beady pinpoint eyes seem to be looking right at me. I was looking intently at him too, as if through a microscope. His eyes looked *huge*. I was hyper-aware of this tiny creature looking at me (like a Lilliputian), not only without any fear but with a look of definite awareness and, I could swear something else, perhaps friendship, or maybe even gratitude. Mr. B seemed to be saying, thanks whoever you are, thanks for picking me up. What a great time we had.

And then something more amazing happened.

As I watched, my vision still acute, he opened his mouth and slowly extended his tongue-like proboscis in a graceful arch to place the tip purposefully on my hand. It was so light I couldn't feel it. Is this how butterflies shake hands? Could we call this cross-species communication? We know it happens with dogs and cats—why not butterflies? I can't prove it, but I'll bet my kayak Mr. B wasn't testing my hand as a food source. That gesture was intentional.

"Did you guys see that?" I ask incredulously.

I'm not sure they had. The whole butterfly thing had been a curiosity to the group. But now they must have thought I was going off the deep end. Christian, though, had taken a personal interest in the little guy too. Later that night, when it was time for Julie and me to head down to the sandbar campsite, he made a safe haven for Mr. B on a tree stump and placed a few drops of sugar water in a bowl. I hoped he'd be safer there than on the river with us.

Despite plenty of room on the sandbar and an open invitation, the others were content to stay close to camp where the logging trucks roared by only thirty yards away. Julie and I took the trail down to the beach by the waterfall, where its simple, hypnotic music lulled us into a long and restful sleep.

I woke at dawn, packed up, and returned to camp before the others were awake to see how the butterfly had fared overnight. But the water bowl sat by itself on the stump. Mr. B had gone and left us without a trace.

Chapter 15

Six people and a 14' raft, Hell Hole rapids, Trinity River
Photo by Serendipity Snapshots

Chapter 16
Karakoram

Fear of all the bad things that might happen has often prevented people from experiencing the greatest things that actually would have happened in their lives.
   —Barbara Dane: from her autobiography
         (to be published soon)

The most dangerous thing you can do in life is play it safe.
   —Casey Neistat The most dangerous thing in life, YouTube video April 22, 2015

The trek from the mountain village of Askole to Concordia along the Baltoro Glacier in Pakistan's Karakorum range is often hailed as the finest in the world. When you reach Concordia at 15,500 feet you are surrounded in a near 360-degree circle by staggeringly high and beautiful snow-covered peaks, including K2, or Godwin Austin as it was once known, the world's second-highest peak at 28,251 feet. Photographer and climber Galen Rowell famously said it is like being in the throne room of the mountain gods. The pyramid of K2 rises like a god among gods, far more difficult and dangerous to climb than the more famed Mt. Everest. Nearby are lesser giants like Gasherbrum I (Hidden Peak), Broad Peak, and the stunningly beautiful Gasherbrum IV, rising like a Himalayan angel, her snow banners often streaming off her flanks, creating an alpine halo. Four of the world's fourteen highest peaks can be seen from Concordia. It had been a lifelong wish of mine to see this place of mountain magic.

No Mere Pastime

Mountaineers and their biographers have created a body of literature in depth and insight unrivaled by any other sport. Indeed, in its uncompromising commitment to attainment, mountaineering seems to rise above the categorization of mere sport. Mountaineers often know the history of their vocation or avocation with deep knowledge and affection. A thousand books would be a conservative estimate that I've read on the subject and my bookshelves bulge with their volumes. With a few calculations one day, I came to this conclusion—that if all the pages from all the books I've read in the genre of mountaineering literature were lined up end to end, they would just about stretch the sixty miles from Askole to Concordia. The stories in these books are not only about the Himalaya, of course, but also about the Andes and the Alps, the Rockies and the Ruwenzori, the Sierra Nevada, and the mountains of South Africa. A hiker on the path that day could read the stirring words of Lionel Terray, the funny and irreverent lines of Tom Patey, heroic stories from Walter Bonatti, the lofty musings of Frank Smythe, and excerpts from the 1,000-page hagiography of the diabolical Aleister Crowley.

Their inspiration has taken me to many ranges in the Western United States, to Canada, to Mexico, and to Europe. But the grandest of all mountain ranges continued to elude my grasp. The great English climber Joe Brown summed up my understanding of Himalayan peak climbing when he described summiting Kanchenjunga, the world's third-highest peak, as 'a long slog'. And there's the rub. I knew in my heart that Himalayan peak climbing was beyond my ability and even desire. I was a crag climber first and foremost, while alpine climbing took second place. Yet my love of mountains was so strong that to be among those great peaks would be fulfillment enough.

Specifically, it was the Karakoram, the other Himalaya, a thousand miles west of the better-known Nepalese Himalaya, that I dreamed of for thirty years. It started when I came across

Chapter 16

Fosco Maraini's *Karakoram*, an account of the first ascent of the beautiful and mesmerizing Gasherbrum IV in 1958 by Italians Walter Bonatti and Carlo Mauri. In retrospect, it was not the actual ascent I remembered (second hand as it was) so much as the approach march through that remarkable country, a march about twice as long as required today.

Maraini's descriptions and photos were vivid, detailed, and compassionate: of the mighty Indus River roiling chocolate brown at flood stage; crossings on swaying footbridges made of plaited tree roots and branches, where a collapse meant instant death; neon green wheat fields of the villages contrasted by the stark hillsides of black rock desert; the tough and sure-footed Baltis who carried heavy loads by day and danced by night; and each little village with its orchards bearing the sweet yellow fruit of apricot trees.

These images would not go away, and I wished to see them for myself, firsthand. Not to top the lofty peaks themselves, but to travel through this land of fable, experience viscerally the gigantic scale of the landscape, to pay tribute as a pilgrim would. But as I approached my 65th year, the window of opportunity seemed to be closing fast.

A lifetime is ultimately a nanosecond in eternity. Many mountains were climbed, many dreams realized, but still, I was no closer to Asia than when I started the journey. A shortage of time, of money, of will, and the global brinkmanship games of fools in power conspired to keep me away. But finally, a window did open. Semi-retirement allowed more time, money was not so short, willpower remained, and only political realities had worsened. Warnings from the State Department, the advice of friends, and concerns of loved ones were the last hurdles. And suddenly, an email arrived in December 2016 from my friend and guide of 35 years, Armin Fisher.

"The trip is on, get ready!"

Armin was determined to go regardless of how small the

party or how slim his profit margin. There would be two parts to this expedition: the trekking portion in which all would participate; and a peak climb which would involve only two of our group. He had dreams to climb something big, perhaps the 26,414-foot Broad Peak. Later, the plan was scaled back to target the regular route on the Great Trango Tower, still no slouch of a peak at over 20,000 feet high. Besides his extensive experience in the United States and Europe, Armin had soloed the 23,000-foot Ama Dablam in Nepal when his clients were incapacitated by altitude sickness.

Suddenly it was real and yet unexpected—a similar plan in 2015 had collapsed. My first reaction was ecstasy. My second reaction, which shortly followed, was doubt about my fitness and ability at 65. I had experienced chronic pain in my right hip and ankle for years. I worried about foreign bugs and getting sick. I worried about my United States citizenship and whether I'd be targeted just for being an American. These fears would dog me throughout the preparation period and well into the trip. But when I consulted Mac, my climbing buddy was emphatic.

"Kenny, if Armin says it's going to be safe, you can count on his word!"

I so wished that the three of us could once again be reunited in a great endeavor but alas, it was not in the cards.

My preparations for Asia were dogged by obstacles from the start, yet they were likely no different than many other parties who must contend with inevitable troubles that attend a big outing. I began in March by gathering a mountain of documents to send off with the visa permit application. The Pakistani consulate had closed recently in San Francisco and the nearest was in Los Angeles. I sent the bulging package off along with my passport, ten dollars' worth of stamps, and a prayer. And waited. And waited some more.

After two weeks I made an inquiry. A gruff and irritated voice on the phone assured me my envelope was not buried

Chapter 16

under a pile of other documents. A call to the Post Office's Los Angeles District Supervisor confirmed the package was lost, midway between the central office and the consulate. It was now April. If it was really lost for good, did I have time to apply for a new passport and then get the visa stamp? The thought of gathering a new Everest of documents made me groan. I wondered if this was a sign I should bow out. One of our crew had done just that, citing age and home responsibilities. Then the package, lost for well over a week, was found—slipped out of sight behind a partition in a mail delivery truck.

Other preparations continued. I needed fleece pants for the cold nights at high altitude, a good 40-liter rucksack, a pee bottle to avoid freezing nighttime out-of- tent experiences, and a giant maroon and tan Patagonia Black Hole Duffel to carry a boatload of gear. I continued to run into one roadblock after another. Armin found a cheap flight from Milan to Islamabad for me but distance and language barriers in dealing with customer relations were a nightmare. I hoped to train at altitude but a massive snowfall in the Sierra prevented hiking at high elevations. From information gathered by reading and a friend who'd been there, our mileage each day would be 6–8 miles. To my consternation, I later discovered that altitude would be a virtual non-factor but our daily hike distances—twice the expected—would prove my greatest challenge.

In late April, my passport arrived stamped with a Pakistani visa but the date of return said July 1, ten days before my flight home. With nervous trepidation and after a touchy call to the gruff civil servant, I sent the passport off a second time to Los Angeles. This time there was no problem with the mail, but the new return date of August 5 was not typed—the old date had been smudged out with a dirty eraser and the new date carelessly penciled in. It looked like a job I could have done myself. I wondered what Pakistani Customs would think of that.

June 12. Departure day arrived and I stepped onto the first

of nine planes that would take me there and back again over the next month. Our British Airways flight over Canada was so rough that the meal service was delayed two hours, while across the aisle someone retched into a paper bag. A five-hour wait between flights was made pleasant at Dublin airport by a service new to me—for 25 Euros you could share a quiet retreat area allowing travelers to catch some shut-eye, purchase food and drinks, and even take a welcome hot shower, all away from the regular hubbub of airport life.

Milan was hot and muggy at 9 PM when Armin picked me up in his Euro van. I'd purposefully arranged a four-day layover in Italy to ease the transition from the United States to Pakistan. I'd be able to rely on Armin, an inveterate world traveler, on my first visit to Asia. We followed the Val Sessia River through innumerable small towns to the tiny village of Riva Del Dobbia under the unseen presence of the monolithic Monte Rosa, at 15,203 feet Switzerland's highest peak. I stumbled uphill over flagstones and grassy slopes in the dark to Armin's snug tile-roofed house and fell into a deep sleep until late morning.

Our days were spent preparing for Pakistan, my nights increasingly troubled and anxious. I started taking sleep aids with mixed results. The chair lifts on the Monte Rosa used by hikers in summer were not operating yet this season, and once again I was unable to train for high altitude. One day Armin took me 'canyoning' on a tributary of the Val Sessia. I'd done a fair amount of canyoneering in the American southwest, but the European version was a different animal.

I stood on the riverbank in my suit of river armor, a full-body wetsuit with outer jacket, neoprene booties, and helmet. Armin was similarly dressed but also had a wetbag with a tether attached to his harness that carried a few supplies. The bag was not designed to keep contents dry, only to keep them together.

Armin had told me virtually nothing about canyoning until now.

Chapter 16

"Keep your feet downstream, let the flow take you around the rocks!"

For the first time, I realized we were going to engage in whitewater kayaking without the kayak. Our bodies *were* the boats.

Armin gracefully floated off downstream with the wetbag in tow, as he should—he'd taken a course to qualify as a canyoning guide. I jumped in tentatively and in the first minute slammed my left hip into a rock. The water was snow-melt cold but my wetsuit kept me tolerably warm. The river was studded with exposed rocks and relaxing was difficult. We got out to walk around a terrifying section called the Devil's Slide. The river slid evilly into a narrow slot, took a right-angle turn, and disappeared into the darkness below. What looked like certain death to me was fun class five kayaking for experts. I was shivering slightly from the cold but also with fear. This was all too new.

Below a large boulder was a deep pool, normally jumped, but I elected to rappel off and release near water level. Armin threw the bag off, jumped, raised his arms overhead, and exhaled just before contact. His friend, also a mountain guide, forgot this procedure at the exact spot once and dislocated his shoulder. My refusal to jump got me in trouble at the next drop off. I lowered slowly to water level, released, but couldn't swim across the strong current to an eddy pool. I was carried toward a small rock-strewn falls where injury was certain. Using familiar rock climbing skills I latched onto a diagonal crack just above water level, pulled myself into a layback position, and held on. Armin needed to relocate to the proper jump off, throw the bag in, jump, cross the current, position on a stable rock, and throw a rescue rope. It was ten minutes before I was safe again.

We passed the last obstacles and took out soon after. My first experience of canyoning had been overwhelming. I'd rather have had a boat between my body and the rocks. Relaxing, I looked around and thought about the contrasts Europe provided every day. Earlier, standing on a footbridge built five centuries ago, we had photographed expert class 5 kayakers negotiating difficult white water. Now, as I carried high-tech outdoor gear following a stone path laid half a millennium ago, the contrast couldn't have been more striking.

Jetlag could only account for part of my sleep disturbance at night. I still struggled with my fears around the upcoming Himalayan experience. This was nothing new—almost every big wall I climbed in Yosemite was preceded by a sleepless night. I told myself to persevere. All of those experiences were now my finest memories.

Every day we drove down-canyon to larger towns for shopping, or to drop Armin's car off for repair, or to buy a Satellite Messenger device that, paired with Armin's iPad, would keep family and friends informed of our progress. Finally, on the last night I slept well, and we rose early for the drive to Milan's Malpensa airport. Several shepherds cajoled a huge herd of goats and some donkeys that were blocking the road. Once past that delay, it seemed all our ducks were lined up, and I felt nothing could go wrong now.

Together we stepped up to airline check-in, placed our baggage on the weighing scale, and presented our passports to a tall, blonde, and officious-looking woman.

"I'm sorry sir but we cannot allow you to board."

"What?" My newly found composure started to shred.

"Your name on the passport doesn't match the name on the ticket. You see, the ticket name is Ken but on your passport it is Kenneth."

I have used those two names interchangeably for decades, in fact, either one is a legal signature, but the woman was having nothing to do with it.

Armin and she had a conversation in Italian to no avail.

With a sinking heart, I pulled the duffel off the scale. We sprinted to a ticketing agency for other options. One flight was

CHAPTER 16

available on Turkish airlines, in four hours. There was no credit for the other flight, and the new one would cost me an extra 900 Euros (nearly a thousand dollars). My original flight had been booked months ago and cost a mere 400 dollars.

Armin tried to reassure me.

"I'll meet you at the airport in Islamabad. Don't worry. My friend Marco is leading a group on the same trek and he's on the same flight as you. Stick with him!"

With that, Armin was gone and I had to wait four hours to board. The problems never seemed to cease. Was this trip jinxed or was it a test? If a test, when does it end? And if jinxed... I pushed the thought away.

Three hours later I met Marco again, having seen him in Alagna by chance earlier in the week. His group was a mix of congenial men and women, Italians mostly, but some Germans. As we approached the gate, I looked for my credit card to make a small purchase. But it was gone, probably dropped during a mad rush at a pizza joint. It was too late to return for a search and I had no secondary card for the trip. Borrowing Marco's phone, I called Julie in California hoping she could report the loss to my credit card company. Then I sank into a chair, glad for new friends, the only barrier right then between me and despair.

Jinx or test? I couldn't think anymore. I found out upon arrival in Islamabad many hours later that Armin in his rush had left his iPad on the ticket counter at the Milan airport.

Islamabad airport buzzed with crowds of people at 4 AM. There was a monstrous heatwave with daytime temperatures high as 115° F, and nighttime temperatures not dropping below the nineties. There was Armin, as promised, standing next to Ingvar, a surgeon from Sweden who would be his climbing partner on the Great Trango. I also meet Mirza Ali, one of the owners of Karakorum Expeditions, the outfit making our trek possible. Mirza was an affable, capable man who didn't mind welcoming strangers at this ungodly hour. In fact, Armin and Ingvar were not strangers, having been clients of Mirza's two years ago for a ski tour in nearby Shimshal.

Armin was excited about the splendid weather in the mountains because it meant we could fly immediately to Skardu without delay. I had hoped to crash into a hotel bed and forget the world for the next twelve hours. It was not to be. Pakistani Airlines would only fly to Skardu in perfect weather, and the rule was never to pass up a chance. It meant we would save at least two days of brutally hard travel over the only other alternative, the infamous Karakorum Highway.

We hung out in a deserted café without air conditioning for the next three hours, me in a twilight zone of stuporous fatigue. Armin was animatedly conversing with Mirza, but I noticed Ingvar looked about as beat as me—a doctor's schedule is never easy. Later we met Bridgette, the only other paying client on our little expedition. She was an attractive British ex-pat living in Amsterdam. Having arrived a day early, she was well-rested and eager to get on with the adventure. She wore traditional local clothing including the hijab, a headscarf. Her nod to local culture would draw admiration and attention from the women and head-turning from the men. I would also find that Bridgette had deep wells of energy and resources to draw from and was infallibly cheerful in any situation.

Many cups of tea and some snacks later, we said goodbye to Mirza and shuffled through customs to the waiting room. A man came over and introduced himself as Hamid, a married man who was serving an eight-month tour of duty in Skardu. It wasn't surprising that he spoke excellent English—Pakistan as part of India until 1948 was an English colony for a hundred years. Hamid explained that India is generally a Hindu country and Pakistan is Islamic—an enormous cultural difference. He graciously welcomed me, wishing me a pleasant and rewarding stay in his home country.

Chapter 16

"Why do not more Americans visit Pakistan?" he wanted to know. "We are not the terrorist country we're made out to be."

I tried to explain that propaganda took many forms and our government was presently hostile to the Islamic world. We both agreed that Donald Trump is a very bad hombre and left it at that.

We talked until it was time to board. I was touched by this man's kindness, sincerity, and willingness to extend himself in friendship to me, a white American whose country has waged war on his people. It would not by any means be the last time I had such encounters in this country of devout Muslims. Just as in Cuba, a country I had the privilege of visiting earlier in the year, the common people have no ill will towards Americans, and we agreed that governments are the problem.

Our 45-minute flight took us past the great bulk of Nanga Parbat (26,660 feet) once known as the Killer Mountain (in the past four decades its death toll has been far surpassed by Mt. Everest). The Skardu Valley is sunk low between twenty-thousand-foot peaks and the plane had to perform descending spirals to lose altitude, like a raptor caught in a downdraft instead of a thermal. The sun beat torrents of heat upon us as we deplaned. Here we met Gul Mohammed, our on-the-ground liaison and one of Karakorum Expedition's owners. He was a compact, athletic, and intelligent man from nearby Shimshal who would make all things possible for the next three weeks. We loaded our gear into a couple of Toyota Land Cruisers and made our way through Skardu's vibrant business district where everything one could want was for sale. It was a hectic scene of cars, trucks, buses, and taxis weaving their way through the crowd of men (very few women were seen) and the occasional cow or donkey, confident of their place here as any human counterpart.

Turning off the main street we came to Concordia Hotel. Stupified by the fatigue of three flights in the last 24 hours, I collapsed into a lounge chair in front of our room. I couldn't yet comprehend my presence on the great continent of Asia, but I was suitably stunned by the commanding view of the Indus River valley. The 16th century Fort Kharpocho perched on a prominent outcrop overlooking the wide, tan watery highway of the Indus River, now in full summer runoff at perhaps 100,000 cubic feet per second. Beyond the desert plain was the fabled Shigar valley, leading to the Braldu River system and the Baltoro glacier. For now, all I wanted was oblivion. Ingvar and I, who shared a room, closed the curtains, turned the ceiling fan on high, and slept the afternoon away.

That evening we dined at the Concordia restaurant where we served ourselves great plates of delicious food, second and third helpings if we wished. Joining us was Frederick, a tall and muscled mountaineer from Sweden, a commanding presence who spoke in long monologues, where getting a word in edgewise was impossible. I met Sir Edmund Hillary once, a huge bear of a man whose hand when I shook it, seemed twice the size of mine. Frederick reminded me of Hillary in that regard only. He was here to attempt K2 with a local climber, Ali. Their plan was a hyper version of 'fast and light', in which they would carry no tents and, after acclimation, make one blitz-like rush for the summit. His diet was singular—no carbs, no gluten, simply protein with liberal amounts of olive oil over everything. He consumed three or four huge plates while regaling us with stories of his exploits, including several attempts on K2.

Later, when Frederick had gone, Gul informed us that the Swede would be joining our group for hiking and meals. We looked around at each other, wondering if our recently bonded little group could survive his overpowering presence.

I walked the darkened streets with a star-filled sky above, listening to strange sounds and smells. A large group of children walked by, talking and laughing. Perhaps they were heckling me like children do, but if so then I didn't mind. I finally felt

Chapter 16

grounded for the first time in Asia. Many of my doubts were now gone but my awe of being in Asia was immense. China was not far to the northeast, India close to the southeast. Iran shared a border to the west and Afghanistan only a few hundred miles to the northwest. There, Trump had just dropped the 'Mother of all Bombs', a stupid and criminal act to my mind. And I'd dropped myself into the biggest adventure of my life, feeling very much alive.

At 3 AM the sharp crackling sound of a loudspeaker system shattered the night quiet and a voice in exotic-sounding Urdu, the official language of Pakistan, intoned prayers for the next hour. It was Ramadan, the holiest holiday of Islam, and the voice reminded all Muslims to rise, pray, and fast. All men, women, and children would eat nothing until dinner the following evening. The projected voice sounded like it could reach into every home in the Skardu Valley.

On our layover day, we visited a tiny studio off the busy main street to have official passport photos taken. Taxi drivers converged on us offering their competing rates when we decided to visit the K2 Museum, where Italy's long-standing connection to this area is highlighted. The victorious 1954 first ascent of K2 is depicted through text, photos, and artifacts. A successful fiftieth-anniversary ascent in 2014 by a group of skilled Pakistani climbers was funded and aided by Italian guides. One of them was a good friend of Armin's from Alagna.

The afternoon found us at Lake Satpara, a couple of thousand feet in elevation outside town for light altitude training. Later we took the ancient weathered stairway to Fort Kharpoccho on Skardu Rock overlooking the Indus River. The heavy wooden entrance doors apparently did not move so we levered ourselves through an awkward opening smack in the middle. Inside, a caretaker greeted us and took a few rupees. The fort was on the decrepit side of ruin, but the view of Skardu in the late afternoon light was magical and we could hear clearly the droning of loudspeaker-assisted prayers for Ramadan far below.

The sole on one of Ingvar's cross-trainer approach shoes peeled away on the return and the best replacement he could find in town were two sizes too big. He'd have to wear double socks for much of the hike. We walked home as the mountains turned a brilliant alpenglow pink. A car detached itself from the busy arterial road and pulled up alongside me. I thought the two men wanted a photo of me but no, they said they'd like me to take a photo of them.

"Show to friends in America." My nationality must have stood out pretty sorely.

"Bring your friends back to visit, we are a friendly country!"

Just before dark, from our porch we watched the people of Skardu make their way home, while above them the poplar trees swayed wildly in the wind, ten feet or more to each side of vertical. Huge cumulus, darkened in the twilight, piled like pillows above the peaks. The weather was changing.

We and our gear were piled high into two Land Cruisers, the vehicle of choice for this leg of the journey. It was going to be a wild ride. As recently as 1958 mountaineers were walking this 54-mile section, adding a week to the journey. After a few miles, one of the Landcruisers had a flat and it was exchanged for a tire seemingly worn smooth of all tread. Once in the valley of the Shigar River, the desert turned green and little villages appeared every few miles. Hand-built, sectioned stone walls delineated each farmer's land. To my Western eye they were incredibly picturesque, the women, their backs turned to us, were harvesting small batches of wheat by hand scythe or drying apricots in the sun. Smiling school children, both boys and girls in crisp uniforms, were walking to school and often waved. We waved back. In one village our temporary liaison Hussein got out to find the best deal for eggs and chickens. I mentally pinched myself, unable to believe I was here, finally, on the road to my dreams.

We passed our last village and in between the Shigar and the

Chapter 16

Braldu river watersheds stopped at a dismal-looking army checkpoint. Gul had to spend a considerable time convincing the guards that we had legitimate papers. I guessed my American passport may have been giving him the most trouble. The weather was humid, overcast, and warm.

Now, on the last part of the day's journey, the drivers' expertise would prove critical. We had left the paved road long ago, and many sections were muddy, narrow, barely wider than the jeep, with drop-offs of a hundred feet or more, leading to a howling Braldu River in full spring melt. If one managed to survive a plunge off the road here, the river would surely finish you off. Nevertheless, our driver never slowed down except when meeting another jeep. Here, they sidled by each other with only a couple of inches to spare. They often stopped to chat and shake hands through the open-windowed vehicle. I took photos and videos of us passing over suspension bridges—only on the return would I find out that this could be grounds for confiscation of my camera.

We came to a high-angled hillside utterly devoid of all vegetation, with loose dirt and rocks ready to dislodge in a slide at any moment. It was here that a landslide had closed the road for months, cleared only a few weeks previously. During the closure, two Landcruisers would be positioned at either end of the closed section, and passengers would walk from one end to the other with their gear, food supplies, medicines, and other necessities. Gul made us disembark and the driver drove on alone.

"Quickly now, run!"

I looked up as I ran, so as to dodge any possible missiles, but the slope was stable for the moment.

Back on board, the driver hounded a solo motorcyclist by tailgating and blasting the horn until he moved aside. The Braldu in flood was unlike any river I have seen in my 65 years. It was an animal—unleashed, angry, and relentless, moving 25–30 miles per hour, a savage, silty brown. House-sized boulders would roll down that unstoppable current. The whole river funneled into a dark and cavernous slot canyon from which nothing could come out alive.

One kayaker braved these waters in the summer of 1984, Andy Embick, a doctor from Anchorage. In his words:

The Braldu had by now, in the second week of June, become more than what is normally called a river, an awesome natural force unleashed, with nightmarish power and violence. Its flow had multiplied 25 times and the truck sized boulders which we had (previously) paddled around were themselves rolling down the river's bed. Bridges, except for a swinging vine rope jhola, were gone as well as was all semblance of being kayakable or survivable....As brown as Karakoram rock and as cold as glacial ice, the Braldu River was the embodiment of death immediate and irrevocable. ...Once, standing awed on the bank, I watched an entire rapid move fifty yards downstream and felt through the earth the reverberation of the rolling boulders. To venture, even briefly out into the probably 30 mph current was to court instant disaster- which I courted- and narrowly escaped.

The same Landcruiser broke down again just before Askole, and once repaired we wound our way up the last rocky hill to town. The view up the valley was like Shangri La. Electric-green terraced fields, rough stone walls, and on either side of the valley, snowy peaks, higher than I'd ever seen, rising 20,000 feet into the sky. The reality of people's existence was in sharp contrast. Their homes were small domed rock hovels, with low entrances, windowless and cheerless. A canal of running water alongside the town path was the sewer. A sad-looking woman with a young child said something pleadingly to me as I passed by. We jostled with a large herd of goats up the path to our campsite, a welcoming large rectangle of grass bordered by young poplar trees. Here, brightly colored tents contained

Chapter 16

expensive down sleeping bags owned by expeditioners wearing clothes and boots equivalent to an Askole family's annual salary.

Ingvar, Armin, Bridgette, and I went for a walk before dinner, mobbed by the village kids chanting "rupees, rupees!" Bridgette knew what to do. In unison she had them raise their arms and leap off the ground together while recording it on her iPhone. When she played it back in slow motion, the kids looked on in wonder.

Children of Askole, Pakistan

That night I was awakened briefly by the chanting of prayers for Ramadan. Normally highly sensitive to noise, I was beginning to adapt to almost anything and finding the droning voice almost soothing. Today, I thought, our first day on the trail should be easy. It would be pure luxury to have most of our gear carried by porters and mules. My 40-liter pack carried only lunch, water, camera, and raingear, no more than fifteen pounds. Overcast and drizzly we shared the trail out of town with goats and their masters. A mile later we officially entered Central Karakoram National Park, highest in the world, and stopped to have the park warden inspect our papers.

Here we learned Frederick was very sick with bloating and cramps. He believed it was gluten poisoning even though the cooks had been given strict instructions to follow his peculiar diet. The upshot was that Frederick insisted on a dedicated cook and mess tent for himself alone. The rest of us were feeling fine and exchanged looks that said, "Well, I guess that issue resolved itself." Frederick eventually stumbled on down the trail yet still kept a pace faster than mine.

We approached a footbridge over the spring melt creek that licked at the underside of the bridge. We all crossed one at a time for safety, but a herd of goats could not be coaxed to do so. I was enjoying walking among these friendly creatures and could imagine the pleasures and challenges of being a goatherd. Wild rose bushes appeared in great numbers sporting enormous blossoms, maybe ten times the size of the native rose in California.

After four hours of hiking, we still hadn't stopped for lunch.

"Gul, how many miles are we hiking today?"

Gul looked thoughtful for many seconds then replied, "I would say about thirty kilometers."

After a quick calculation, I said, "Thirty? Are you kidding? That's about eighteen miles!"

Next to me, Bridgette did not look as surprised as I must have.

Chapter 16

As we walked on I didn't know what to think but later realized Gul was using an old psychological trick—give a client a large number and then have him pleasantly surprised when it's less. But what he didn't realize was that I had expected half-day marches. That day's march and many others would come to around 12 to 14 miles, twice what I'd expected.

We stopped for lunch at Korophon, a wide, flat area where several mild streams converged. It is near the toe of the Biafo Glacier which, if followed, would lead to the fabled and now deeply troubled kingdom of Kashmir. A light but steady rain fell and made unpacking the mules for lunch a problem, so we ate boiled potatoes, tea, and some cookies. For supplement, I broke out the first of two-dozen food bars from my personal stash, knowing too well the limitations of my low body-fat index and high metabolism.

Armin kept me company as I lagged behind the others through the early afternoon. Sheer rock walls lined the Braldu and we traveled a mile through a spectacular half-tunnel dynamited by the Pakistani Army. This section once required a long detour over the mountaintop above. The Braldu is wide and braided with occasional brilliant white boulders looking like mid-river icebergs as the sun briefly breaks through. The tunnel section ended at the Dumordo River where at low water one could wade across and save several kilometers of hiking. No chance of that this day. Soon we saw across the river a strange grouping of perhaps two dozen small gray 'huts'. This was Jhula, our first camp. The huts were actually outhouses and shower stalls funded by the Italian alpine club.

The rope bridge that used to cross the river and gave the camp its name had been replaced by a solid wooden structure another mile upriver. I groaned inwardly as the sight of camp receded, knowing we'd have to walk the same distance back on the other side. The others had been in camp an hour when I stumbled in and gratefully accepted a folding chair, hot soup, and chapattis. Then the weather started to close in—Jhula has a reputation for high winds and rainy conditions. I crawled into my tent and slept until dinner, a pattern I would have to follow most of the trip to recover from daily exertions.

At dawn, I awoke refreshed to a world bright and cheerful, for the all-night rain clouds had dispersed to reveal a stunning sight—the snowy peak of 20,629-foot Mango Gusor, seemingly driving its summit halfway to the sky's zenith. Jhula was bustling with parties from around the world, their porters and mules weaving their way through mud puddles as they left on the day's journey. The gray outhouses, all with a crescent moon symbol on the door, were in various stages of repair but had done good service to improve hygiene at camp. Some porters swept animal dung to the side of the path.

Geoff, our cook, kept us well fed with fresh eggs, potatoes with vegetables, and tea; to pack in more calories we slathered chapattis with peanut butter and an Italian chocolate/hazelnut concoction called Nutella. This should be an easier day, and I expected to perform better, but only a mile from camp a headache came on quickly and unexpectedly. Soon the others outdistanced me and Armin patiently stayed behind. Our trail for the morning was hardpacked rock and dirt, with a gentle rise in elevation. We left the trail at one point to walk among the cobbles in a dry riverbed. A cliff of massive, barely consolidated cobbles towered a hundred feet overhead.

By noon, six hours later, there was no sign of our party. I had eaten all of my snacks and part of Armin's too. Armin could trek all day like a camel without food or water if necessary. I was craving calories. Long distances and high elevation were one thing, but a missed lunch, now that was serious. I feared the others had left us behind for our next camp, Paiyu.

At 1:30 PM the little 'settlement' of Bardumal appeared. It had a spring and a small hut where an old man and his grandson were caretakers for the summer. And here we found our

Chapter 16

party fed and ready to depart. Gratefully, almost tearfully, I sat in the lee of a boulder and consumed a boiled potato, boiled egg, cheese, and cookies. Massive snow-topped peaks marched up the valley on both sides like advancing armies. As we left camp, the old man was devoutly performing his prayers to Allah.

Now the trail was demanding all of our attention. We crossed alluvial fans up to a mile or two wide, consisting of vast fields of stream outflow boulders, a chaotic jumbled scene where the trail divided and divided again into multiple tracks. Numerous streams had to be crossed sometimes by rock hopping, sometimes by crude wooden bridges of planks secured by large rocks on either end. Once we hiked down into and out of a steep defile, 100 vertical feet high, every step loose and ready to slide.

By late afternoon Armin was carrying my pack as well as his. The shadows lengthened across the wide Braldu River far below. Looking to exchange my sunglasses for regular lenses, I found the black case in the top pocket of my pack gone, slipped out somehow and swallowed up by the rocky terrain. Fortunately, a second older pair, included as an afterthought, was buried in the Patagonia Black Hole duffel.

Finally at 5 PM, after twelve hours of hiking, we came to Paiyu, a surprising tree-shaded camp with good water, perched on terraces high above the river. Orange, red, yellow, blue, and green tents of Japanese, Canadian, Australian, and Pakistani parties lent a festive air to the place. Our tents, pitched hours ago, were on a flat terrace next to the stream. Above was a ranger hut, the ceiling of which was also used for camping. Down the hillside were another collection of gray outhouses and shower stalls. It was too late for an afternoon nap and I was too tired to sleep anyway. Happy to have come this far, my headache had dissolved with a couple of quarts of water, and tomorrow was a layover day. If I made it to Concordia it would be a young man's dream accomplished by a senior.

We ate a lavish dinner in our mess tent and played cards into the early evening. Geoff was up late cleaning pots and preparing for the next day. He was a quiet man of talent, going about his work unassumingly. Armin had great respect for him, as we all did. He would keep us not only well-fed but healthy, and my fears of stomach ailments were soon banished. A generator went off at nine and the camp of perhaps a hundred souls was silent.

Our layover day was a day to bask in luxury. I washed clothes, wrote in my journal, and marveled to simply be there. Armin, Bridgette, and Ingvar scrambled high above camp towards Paiyu Peak and later reported of far-off views of K2 and Broad Peak.

That morning a group of climbers from Chile were off for an attempt on K2. A Slovenian was with them, planning on a ski descent of the regular route. A group of North Korean women arrived at camp later. It was exciting to meet people of different races and cultures, to exchange ideas and information, and where mutual support was offered. Climbers form an international community of their own and nationalistic fervor is rare. Here was a model for world governments to emulate. I was reminded of a quote by Walter Bagehot, "Nations touch at their summits."

Next to the little community of gray outhouses was a cement basin with a water tap. Here I soaped up and rinsed for a first bath since Skardu. Knowing the cultural injunction against public nudity, I made sure to keep some underwear on. The porters, if they washed, would have the advantage of their shalwar, a long flowing shirt that also serves Islamic modesty requirements. I noticed though that Gul, who was more westernized, washed up like I did.

In clear, late-afternoon light, Bridgette and I walked down to the 'lake', an overflow body of water created by the river in flood stage. In the distance, one of the North Korean women was looking for bathing privacy. Paiyu Peak came into full view, a fantasy castle of a mountain with multiple towers, flying buttresses,

Chapter 16

ridges, and deep couloirs—a massive birthday cake of a mountain with snow frosting on top. Close beyond that were the Trango and Cathedral groups, like alpine saw teeth raking the sky. On the other side of the glacial valley were the Masherbrums. No superlative language, no photographs could convey the enormity of the scale here or the pure gravitas of being among these earth giants. You must be there in person to understand.

The night was warm, way too warm as we played Gin Rummy and Hearts in the mess tent after dinner. Tomorrow was going to be a scorcher.

Armin's wakeup call came at 4 AM but already the eastern horizon was paling with new light. That night I had zipped my sleeping bag down and laid it over like a blanket, yet I was still too warm. Paiyu Camp was at 12,000 feet. How high did we have to go for alpine chill?

Landscape contrasts were stark—we walked through a barren desert of black rock and scree slopes while all around towered snow-covered 20,000–23,000-foot peaks. As we approach the snout of the Baltoro Glacier, a trail branched off and a small handmade sign with an arrow stated 'Trango'. We continued on the main trail, a steep climb over shifting sands and rocks nearly hiding the fact that we were climbing the toe of the glacier. The Baltoro was unlike any glacier I'd ever seen. You had to look closely under piles of rock debris to discern its true nature, revealed now and then by scarps of black-fringed ice. From my view at the top of the scarp, the Braldu River emerged from the bottom of the glacier, frothing brown with sediment, bursting forth as a river fully born, like Athena from the head of Zeus. The 200-foot-high scarp had nearly continuous rockfalls and earth slumps pitching down its sides. I stood back a healthy distance from the crumbly edge to avoid becoming part of this geology lesson in mass wasting.

The 'trail' wended its way over chaotic jumbles of large and small stones and occasional huge boulders. The Baltoro is one of the few stable glaciers in the world and not diminishing due to climate change. It seems that the thick cover of rocky debris serves as an insulator. Gul and Bridgette were moderating their normally faster pace for me today while Armin and Ingvar were far ahead. Gul took us on a short cut through a parallel stream course to the right of the main glacier. Blocked by a waterfall we ascended a steep hillside with some class II and III scrambling. Most of the porters and all the mules had to take a longer, slower but easier route.

By now the heat was stupefying. I asked Gul how hot he thought it was. Wrong question. He looked at his iPhone and reported 46° C. Bridgette translated that to 113 ° F. I hoped Gul was playing psychological games again but if not, this set a new personal record. I sat down in the paltry partial shade of a rock and insisted on eating a boiled potato and crackers despite the heat. The others were not hungry.

Later we hurried past a high, unstable cliff face that Gul said could slide at any moment. Our trail had converged with the main trail now and far below we saw mules and people crossing a tributary stream without the benefit of a jhula (rope bridge). The crossing was only 30–40 feet across but knee to thigh high. The three of us linked arms for safety. When a porter loaned me his shoes I tied my boots to the pack. They looked like a pair of Crocs, pretty standard attire for porters. Yet the porters were agile as mountain goats and I'd never seen one make a misstep. By the end of the short crossing, my feet and legs were screaming with the pain of the ice water. It was hard to believe anything this cold could still be liquid. Even a waist-high crossing twice this width of the Popo Agie River in the Wind River Range of Wyoming at spring melt had been more tolerable.

Another hour of climbing uphill in the heat brought us to Khoburtse, our scheduled lunch stop. It was nearly mid-afternoon and Urdukas our destination was three hours beyond.

Chapter 16

"Armin, if you find a mule to carry me I can go on, but otherwise I'm done!"

After a conference, it was decided to stay for the night. Tomorrow we would go past Urdukas to Goro I to stay on schedule. I tried to nap in the tent but the heat was too intense. As soon as the sun sank behind Paiyu Peak though, it started to cool and I welcomed the hard-won elevation gain. A sharp-eyed Balti had spotted mountain goats on the hillside above camp. It was here in 1958 that Ricardo Cassin, leader of the Italian Gasherbrum IV expedition, went off to hunt for mountain goats and misjudged the distance. He had to spend a freezing night without shelter to the worry of his companions, yet survived without injury.

Our camp, like Paiyu Camp, was a series of terraces, but without the benefit of shade, trees, or toilet facilities. Yet it sported incredible views of the Baltoro Glacier, Paiyu Peak, Trango, and Cathedral peaks. Despite the crowding and lack of sanitation, I quickly grew fond of this site. There was a pipe with flowing water where a cold bath could be had. That night we would feel the first real chill of the alpine world. Though rock covered, the Baltoro's thick ice reserves were providing a natural air conditioning, so from then on, I would be sleeping inside a fully zipped bag.

In the dawn chill, I walked out of camp looking for privacy, oddly at a premium here in this vast wilderness of rock and ice. The traditional clothing of a Muslim affords a built-in privacy screen, but we Westerners had to either forget modesty or search farther. I was of the latter persuasion, passing feces piles everywhere until finding a suitable site.

Snowy Paiyu Peak and the Great Trango obelisk lorded it over lesser summits down-valley, while ahead lay calamitous heaps of boulders, rocks, and scree that seemed intent on turning an ankle. Side canyons showed tortured ice falls below peaks of blindingly white snowfields. Ephemeral so-called mushroom rocks appeared, boulders weighing many tons supported precariously on lumps or columns of snow. The boulders themselves had created their own altars by slowing ice melt underneath while all around the snow had melted out. Long, thin meltwater lakes inhabited hollows, tinted blue-green by glacial till. Another mini fjord with less sediment in the water showed sky blue. We had entered the wonderland that photographer Vittorio Sella in 1906 called "the world's most amazing museum of forms and shapes."

For Fosco Maraini in 1958, this leg of the trip was torture. He "envied the very stones...nothing urged them on and on...nothing disturbed their place in the sun."

> *It seemed one of those endless treks. There was always one more mound of stony stuff to climb or circumnavigate. Not a hundred meters of plain sailing. No peace for your feet and your legs. It was one long climb with stepping stones thrown in—huge block-like stepping stones, and stream after stream between them. There were crevasses to be on the lookout for and shifting sand that you tried to grab at with your feet. Sometimes there were long, stiff climbs. But when you got to the top it was only the top of some puny hillock, though you thought you had gained a great height. Then on the other side you had to go down, down once more, to the bottom of the trough. Measured in actual foot-slogging I think this particular day's march would show twice the mileage one would infer from the map.*

Another meltwater lake appeared, this one tan brown with heavy sediment load. Ice scarps fringed chocolate brown are many—these are scenes of entertainment for resting hikers to watch a nearly continuous cascade of rocks and sand sliding down their slopes into the meltwater lakes.

High on the mountainside, we spotted an oasis of green contrasting with white granite. This was Urdukas, for many peak

Chapter 16

climbing aspirants the last greenery they would see for months. Mansion-size boulders perched on wildflower-strewn, grassy hillsides, watered by rushing ice-melt streams. Urdukas means fallen boulders and was indeed a reminder of the danger inherent in this environment. Some years back, a house-sized boulder split in two killing three porters in their camp. We lunched on the tip of a massive promontory of rock looking across the valley at the Great Cathedral, over 19,000 feet high yet devoid of snow except on its horizontal ledges. Urdukas is the favored stopover for unladen porters returning from K2 base camp. They can make the trek of sixty miles in two days, the same distance we would take most of a week to do.

As we left Urdukas we passed a Pakistani army camp of three white dome huts looking like modules from some futuristic space movie. Then it was back to the glacier. Ever since Askole we'd been seeing thin black cable lines lying in the dirt, or half-buried in rocks, or even draping like clotheslines down the faces of some ice scarps. These were the ruins of a telephone line constructed by the Army, connecting their camp at Goro III just short of Concordia. It worked for only a few years until the inexorable movements of the Baltoro glacier brought it all down. Now the wooden supports that held the lines were used by porters for campfires.

Topping one of the endless rises, we saw a nearly triangular white blade thrust its way heavenward. From first sight, I fell in love with Gasherbrum IV, (G4) 26,001 feet high. Its north and south ridges rose a full 6,000 feet from its base while the wind-blown snow, usually seen as a banner off the tops of Himalayan peaks, was creating a white fringe around the entire peak. The whole effect felt like a Himalayan angel in full raiment.

A thunderous sound to my left drew my attention to a dust cloud indicating a massive rockslide. The cloud of pulverized rock dust continued to grow and hang in the air for the half-hour it took for it to pass out of view. Slate greys, ash whites, and brick reds make up the palette of stones we walked upon. At times streams gushed forth from the rock stratum and ran over the surface, carving channels of varying depth. At one difficult place, the glacial melt had undercut a bank by several feet. Here we had to step upon a stone mid-channel and leap to the other side with a helping hand. For some small distance, this channel looked like fun for a kayaker, only to disappear into a cave and continue its underground course. Likely no kayaker or hiker swept in could survive the frigid water or ever emerge again from this river Styx.

I came upon the comical sight of Bridgette using a seat-shaped, scalloped ice formation for a rest. The terrain was a bit smoother to walk now and dotted by finely carved heaps of snow, each formation with a steep face and easier backside. These I was told were *penitentes,* formed through uneven melting of the snow. I was familiar with this geomorph, or earth form, in the Sierra where they form a matrix on snowfields of scalloped divots one to three feet deep. But each of these formations I was looking at were 50 to 75 feet high. Maraini mentions these also:

> *Here and there, we came across pyramids of neve, hard and compact, fifty or sixty feet high. These formations, which have been called the 'Sails of the Baltoro', crown the stoney stratum... which covers the ice and probably marked the last outposts of powerful spring avalanches.*

According to recent scientific research, Maraini's idea is not correct. It seems that when rocky debris first falls on the ice, solar radiation increases and the ice begins to melt. Bare ice is more reflective, melts slowly, and thus appears to rise as the main ice body lowers. But then, when the rock debris continues to build from the mountainsides, an insulation layer builds up and slows melting, and it's the turn of the *penitentes* to melt faster. Some

Chapter 16

penitentes can last decades, maybe a hundred years. The low humidity helps create a unique environment for these formations, for they are found nowhere else in the world. *Penitentes* often cluster together on long, flat stretches of glacier where they can ride down-valley in glacial slow motion. They are not seen where the land rises and falls—there they would be destroyed too quickly.

A cloud banner formed across the upper face of G4. We stopped at Goro I, an informal camp where we helped the porters smooth out tent sites. Our stay here and on the return would be the only time we would have a camp to ourselves. There were two stone-walled, roofless structures that the porters would house in for the night, draping tarps over the top and huddling together for warmth. The mules were led to some sparse grazing far up the mountain. The mules could not carry feed as well as gear and so ate very little in the upper elevations. Some mules, tough as they are, do not survive the trip, not from lack of food, but the intense night cold, according to Gul.

When night fell the stars were brilliant, it was blessedly quiet and a fine chill filled the air.

Concordia was only a day's march away and by now I realized with excitement that my dream was within reach. Barring a catastrophe, I was going to make it. Ingvar has been feeling poorly the last two days, but his pace only slowed down to mine on a good day. The phantasmagoria of geomorphic shapes continued. One large *penitente* (the word comes from penitent, a religious devotee seeking heaven) had a beautiful fringe at its base, decorated like the hem of a dress.

We climbed a steep, high pass in the vicinity of Mustagh Tower, hidden that day by clouds, and lunched on top. The Mustagh is a commanding matterhorn of a peak, first climbed in 1955 by Brits Joe Brown and Ian McNaught Davis. My 1972 first edition of Brown's autobiography, *The Hard Years*, shows Brown on the cover, resting at the base of that impossible-looking tower of rock and ice, with a lit cigarette in his hand (legend has it he smoked a celebratory cig on the 23,871-foot summit). The modest Brown gave only a short chapter in his book to that amazing success story.

In between passing mule caravans, Armin challenged the group to a rock-throwing contest—"let's see who can hit that big white boulder down-slope." That was a red flag for me —I spent many hours of my boyhood throwing rocks for distance and accuracy. But it was Gul who nailed it first, crediting his prowess to time spent hunting. I hit the target later but no one else came close.

Whole communities of rocks balanced on ice pedestals greeted us farther down the trail. It was a warm day and even the frigid, glass-clear stream-melt rivers were inviting me to take a dip. But when I mentioned my daily cold plunges at this altitude in the High Sierra, Gul warned me off.

"Much too cold, the shock could make you sick."

Our elevation was around 14,000 feet now, near the maximum height of the Sierra Nevada crest, but here we hadn't even reached the base of these Karakorum giants. Imagine two Sierra Nevada ranges stacked one atop the other! The elevation was not a factor in my fatigue, only the long distances over uneven terrain. Later in the day, I was so tired that I was unable to walk in the proper sense of the word, only stagger, and Armin was carrying my pack again. I saw people and a camp on the horizon, but it was only Goro III, the Pakistani Army camp with more space-age white domes. A shocking amount of litter, dung, and human waste littered the camp's stony hillocks.

Almost reading my mind, a man in uniform shouted, "Only one hour more." I waved in thanks but knew for me it could be twice that. We passed a mummified mule with pack gear still strapped around the midsection of the carcass. It wouldn't be the last time we would see such a sight.

Turning a corner, we saw Bridgette sitting on a small, accom-

Chapter 16

modating *penitente*, waiting for the slowpoke (me). Finally, a red tent on the next hill came into view and, at the last minute, K2 itself. I was exhausted but upright, and decidedly ecstatic to be here. The porters pitched our yellow North Face VE 24's with the doors facing K2 and Broad Peak, the second and twelfth highest peaks in the world. To the right of Broad Peak was G4, my lodestone, now a gargantuan pyramid of snow and ice.

Few ascents have been made since 1958 of G4, a climb harder than K2. A 1985 ascent of the west face was deemed by *Climbing Magazine* the greatest Himalayan climb of the 20th century. G2 shyly peeked around its shoulder and just out of sight was G1 or Hidden Peak, the only 8,000-meter peak first ascended by Americans. Golden Throne was to its right, then Baltoro Kangri, Shisapangma (14th highest peak in the world), Chogolisa just out of sight, and towering directly behind us, the lance-like Mitre Peak. Except for the glacially carved valley of the Baltoro, we were virtually surrounded by some of the highest peaks in the world. I could admire this view forever. And indeed, tomorrow I would sit in my chair by the mess tent all day, do nothing, and consider it one of the greatest mountain days of my life.

The air turned cold at night, but worse was the cold seeping upward through hundreds of feet of glacial ice right through the tent floor, thin pad, and sleeping bag. The thick green foam pad I'd been using was elsewhere that night. I put on all my clothes, three layers on top, fleece pants, my best thermal socks, a down vest over my feet (and to insulate the camera batteries). I slipped a rain jacket over the foot of my bag, an old trick I learned sleeping in a snow cave on Mt. Lassen. Then with a woolen hat on my head and cocooned inside the fully zipped Marmot I finally reached 'warm'.

The porters' tumbledown rock shelter with a portable tarp for a roof had gaps in the rock walls stuffed with ammo cans, cardboard, or other material. They had no sleeping bags but huddled together for warmth with perhaps a blanket or two to drape over them. In the early morning hours, I was awakened by the loud moaning of a porter. As tough as the Baltis were they were not immune to the vicissitudes of this harsh life. I felt incredibly spoiled. Yet the cold was intense and I would not even venture out to take a pee. Carefully, I nearly filled a 16-ounce plastic bottle with urine, replaced the cap tightly, and placed it securely upright in the tent's corner for good measure. Back in Italy, Armin had noticed my 12-ounce recycled peanut-butter jar intended for this service and advised me to buy something larger. That was good advice.

The night chill waned quickly with the sun. It was a gorgeous day, a Technicolor dream. Gul, Armin, and Bridgette would hike to K2 base camp. They wanted to visit the Art Gilkey memorial and Armin would scatter ashes of his sister and my friend Tanja, who died too young at 42. I needed to rest—the next day we were due to turn around and do it all over again. Ingvar had decided to layover also and save his strength for the upcoming Great Trango climb. I was content to watch the unparalleled panorama around me most of the day, photographing, reading, journaling, or washing socks. Geoff cooked us delicious samosas, four apiece for me and Ingvar. Ingvar was a naturally quiet man and though we'd been sharing a tent we hadn't spoken much. Now we got to know each other. He was a surgeon in Sweden who also did research at Lund University. His responsibility was great and he had that doctor's serious mien. He spoke in a low, quiet voice of authority. An occasional smile really lit up his face.

His travels had taken him to Borneo, Alaska, Japan, California, and the Rockies. His strengths were as an alpine skier and mountaineer but not so much pure rock climbing. He had climbed some major alpine routes in his younger days and I got the feeling that, like me, he was nostalgic for the times when he could blast up big routes at high speed.

Downslope, I visited the metal-stepped, canvas-walled out-

Chapter 16

house with a hole in the floor's center and a blue 55-gallon barrel underneath. They apparently just seal it up and pack it out on a mule. I wandered slowly back to camp admiring a rainbow variety of stones underfoot—red, green, pink, white, yellow, black, and gray. A couple of the nicer ones were coming home with me.

Cloud streamers cleared off K2 and by afternoon we had an unobstructed view of the region's five-mile-high monarch. We were incredibly lucky again with the weather—many parties camp for days at Concordia in clouds and whiteout. By sunset I was still in a t-shirt, madly shooting pictures with both cameras. Golden alpine glow flooded the west face of G4 while black shadows engulfed its base. A cloud cap formed over the top of K2 indicating a weather change tomorrow.

Captain Sana, who we met at Paiyu Camp, was the Army liaison officer for all peak-climbing parties. He would join us for dinner. Captain Sana was an affable, talkative man, thrilled to have this post, which would last most of the summer and he hoped next summer too. His unfortunate porter had lost a mule down at Paiyu and had to carry most of the Captain's possessions on his back. It was a great loss for the Balti—to purchase another mule would cost a summer's wages. He seemed to be taking it in his stride.

The cold gathered quickly but it had been too fine a day to retire. We stood outside the tents shivering a bit and admiring the crescent moon behind the Mitre and the sky black as space itself. A fire flickered.

"Geoff, did they carry the wood up on mules?"

"No," said our cook, "it is a bit of rubbish and bamboo poles that once supported the telephone line. Come, we can sit by it."

One of our porters, Sher Mohammed, who had been feeding the blaze, found chairs and crates for us to sit on. We gathered around and Captain Sana translated as we asked questions of our porter. Sher Mohammed was 50 years old with fine, even features, a handsome man with a certain noble gravity. He carried loads all summer for hikers and climbers like us, as he has for the past 30 years. To me he had a look of contentment, accepting life as it is. I marveled that he radiated health despite carrying these punishing loads on one of the most difficult approaches in the Himalaya.

"What is your secret to health?" I asked Captain Sana to translate.

Sher Mohammed replied simply, "The exercise of my work."

We were joined by two younger men who had just returned from fixing ropes over the Gondogoro La, a high pass leading to the Hushe Valley, an alternate loop return to Skardu for trekkers. Marco's group, a day behind us, would be happy to hear this news.

I took a moment to look up at the stars, to pinch myself metaphorically and remind myself where I was. Here, in the middle of Asia, in one of the wildest places in Asia, warming ourselves around a fire, a circle of companions I didn't know even a week ago, to feel safe and content in the heart of the Karakorum and Islamic Pakistan, and to feel the goodwill of these fine people, this I will never forget.

The green foam pad was back in my tent that night to stop the cold seeping from the bottomless ice tomb below. The next day we started our return.

Our hike back to Goro II would be the easiest of the trip. The high peaks were still clearly visible that morning, but clouds were quickly filling the valleys below them. The weather was changing fast. We met Marco's trekking party early on, first the advance contingent then the slower group. One man in the slow group was very sick and he would have to be evacuated by mule. Only the advance group would see the high peaks at Concordia before clouds and storm moved in for the duration of their stay there.

Half of the Mustagh Tower was visible for me this time but,

Chapter 16

despite the hour it took to pass it, I was denied a full view of the peak by lowering clouds. Our early arrival allowed us to luxuriously lay around until 3 PM when the others caught up. It was decided to stay there for the night since they had done a double march from K2 base and were thrashed. Bridgette had developed a nasty set of blisters. She was so cold the night before that she moved into the mess tent with others for warmth. Clouds moved swiftly down the valley obscuring the sky, winds blew the goraks tumbling through the sky and by evening it was raining.

By morning poor Bridgette had developed a cold too but despite these setbacks was nearly cheery as ever. I had never seen anyone with such a positive attitude. Born in England but living in Amsterdam, she worked for Doctors Without Borders traveling around the world on business. At home, she rode her bicycle everywhere and for vacation did motorcycle trips around Europe, sometimes solo.

It was difficult getting back to Khoburtse while intermittent rain fell all day. We spotted our third dead mule of the trip, facedown in a glacial meltwater pond. Not a stirring sight. At Urdukas, the sick member of Marco's party seemed happy to be riding out. A wise move since the Gondogoro La is 18,000 feet high and more difficult than anything on the Baltoro. Later I heard about a man and his son in another party who also cut their trip short due to the challenges. Altitude is fickle and can affect a person regardless of fitness or age. I cautioned myself not to get too prideful of my performance as a senior out here. At Paiyu we would meet a large party of Japanese elders in their sixties and seventies doing the same hike.

Despite cloudy and cool weather at Khoburtse, Gul, Armin, Ingvar and I washed up at the piped water outlet. I had no idea what arrangements Bridgette had made. Most of us kept partially covered during the bath, but Ingvar the Scandinavian had no such compunctions and stripped naked for his wash. I noticed one old man glaring at Ingvar, a dark scowl on his face, really giving him the evil eye. Ingvar did not seem to notice.

The following day we were pioneering new ground by making a shortcut crossing of the Baltoro glacier over to Trango base camp. Even Gul had not been this way. Most of the porters and all the mules made the long circuit nearly back to Paiyu before heading up the branch trail to Trango. The mule trail up the Baltoro was about equivalent to high-altitude cross-country travel in the Sierra, perhaps harder at times, since most Sierra talus fields are more stable. Now, doing actual cross country on the Baltoro, with its totally unconsolidated talus and scree deposits in constant flux, we reached another level of difficulty altogether.

As I floundered in quicksand-like scree Armin said, "Follow exactly in my footsteps."

The temporary consolidation of the steps was helpful.

At one nasty spot, I saw our two porters, one being Sher Mohammed, patiently waiting ahead on a steep slope, carrying 55-pound loads. Ice scarps hundreds of feet high stained dark by sediments must be skirted on Baltoro's ridges, the ponds of frigid meltwater at their bases to be avoided at all costs. To fall in meant instant hypothermia, especially on this overcast day. Gul was like a kid in his element, scouting ahead through the chaotic landscape. Per his instructions, we waited while he found the best route, then he signaled us to follow from a distant ice scarp. Several hours of this halting progress took us to the far side of the glacier, solid ground, even some wildflowers, and a snack break.

Now we had to negotiate a steep canyon with the Trango glacier on the left and a massive rock wall on the right. There was a chance the rock wall would stop our progress before we connected with the trail high above. If so, we'd have to make a long, exhausting, and discouraging detour. It would make the day worse than if we'd just gone with the porters from Khoburtse.

Chapter 16

I cringed at this thought. We waited for word from the advance party over lunch. Then, good news. A route had been found or, as I found later, partially forged.

The cliff face did indeed pinch off access after an exposed traverse on unstable ground. We detoured down a steep, rocky gully to the glacier itself. We crossed by hopping across rocks spanning a large meltwater pond, stepping quickly due to highly unstable slopes above that threatened rockslides, and which we saw and heard nearby. The rocks we stepped across, the key to the route, had been placed by Gul, Armin, and the two porters.

Just beyond was the regular trail. The main group of porters, despite covering many more miles, had caught up with us, leading the mules and a black and white Billy goat, destined for the cook pot tonight. I was the last to top the rise and look into the beautiful and spectacular Trango Base Camp. On the right was the impossibly high Great Trango Tower (20,623 feet), whose summit was 6,000 feet above us, twice the height of Yosemite's El Capitan. The camp basin itself was inviting, nearly level, a large lake at its far end was flanked by a mirror-smooth granite wall hundreds of feet high. Near the lake were three colorful red and purple tents belonging to the only other party here. Only about six parties a year make it to Trango. One expedition leader with 30 years' experience on the Baltoro told me he'd never had the chance to visit Trango.

On the left was the Trango Glacier, a labyrinth of twisted ice, deep crevasses lined up back-to-back at right angles to the direction of ice travel, and constant rockfall. I'd never seen a glacier this active close up. Reports I'd read of constant rumblings and cracklings of ice and rockslides had not been exaggerated.

We soon met the only other party here. Rolf was a professional mountain guide from Australia and his client Matt was from Scotland. They were here to climb the same route on the Great Trango as Armin and Ingvar. They invited us to a lovely lunch inside their mess tent. Some chickens scratched around outside the tent.

The standard joke on these expeditions went:

"What are the names of those chickens?"

"Well, that one's called Monday, this one's Tuesday, over there is Wednesday and his friend is Thursday."

I went off to catch some afternoon shuteye before dinner. Later in the night, I woke to the soothing patter of raindrops on the tent.

The morning dawned brilliantly clear. The Uli Biaho range, with many still unclimbed summits, was reflected flawlessly in the basin's lake, its snowy summits floating high above inviting granite towers. Our layover day provided Armin and Ingvar the time to prepare for their climb of the Great Trango, by sorting gear and readying the new Bibler tent.

We said goodbye to Matt and Rolf who headed off on their climb. In the afternoon a cliff face near camp provided some sporty rock climbing for the group. I found the 14,000-foot elevation slowed me down on a moderate 5.8 crack. Gul, who had never climbed rock before, proved a natural talent and was pleased to complete the climb. We invited the porters to try but they only smiled and declined. Colossal masses of cumulus cloud boiled over peaks to the south, flying past 23,000-foot peaks. The golden afternoon light illuminated the Trango Towers like cathedrals. We took group photos under the Great Trango—it was our last day together as a group. Afterward, I had a few moments alone to soak in the afternoon's last warmth, to savor how small I was in the vastness, and to be grateful for life. Goraks croaked their way across the lower wall of the Great Trango, its face touted as the highest cliff in the world.

Tomorrow Armin and Ingvar would start up the huge gully toward the peak. Geoff was staying behind to cook for them and Gul joked there would be no more food until we reached Askole three days march away. Our farewell dinner was a delicious goat

Chapter 16

soup. At midnight I went out to take a pee (yes, the weather was warmer here) and saw the bulk of the Great Trango, a shadowed silhouette, so big it seemed to blot out most of the night sky.

Under the Nameless Tower, Trango Basecamp
Top L-R: Bridgett Simpkins, Gul Muhammad, Ingvar Syk
Bottom L-R: the author, Armin Fisher

In the morning we parted and wishing our friends the best of luck took the porter trail across the Trango Glacier. It was like being in the bowels of some beast, with all the attendant gurgles and groans as it digested its meal of ice and rock. A long, sandy descent to the Baltoro brought us to a veritable Eden with warmer temperatures, greenery, and flowering plants including wild rose. We were obliged to cross the Baltoro a second time when our trail was cut off by the tumbled snout of the glacier, only this time it was nearly flat and far, far easier.

I declined politely while Gul and Bridgett partook in a grisly-looking portion of goat's head for lunch. Approaching Paiyu the withering heat returned. Without our cook Geoff, Gul would have to improvise. Fortunately, a cousin of his was in camp, also leading a trek and we were loaned his excellent chef for the night. He cooked a different themed meal each day and that night it was Chinese.

The next day I managed to keep up with my companions and Gul remarked I must have been getting stronger. I was flattered for a moment, then realized Bridgette's blistered feet on top of being sick and Gul's poor night's sleep had simply leveled the playing field. At Bardumal I said hello to the old hut keeper and asked in vain if someone had turned my glasses into 'lost and found'.

Jhula was nearly deserted this time and our porters had selected the best site in camp. It was next to the ranger hut and a large rectangle of open space encircled by young poplar trees. We even had tables and chairs to sit in with a piped spring nearby. It felt like paradise. Mango Gusor was entirely visible to the south and an autumn-like wind was blowing the leaves in the trees. For the first time, I felt a surplus of energy after a full day's hike and eschewed my afternoon nap.

It turned out Gul was not kidding about the food situation. The porters and he scavenged some old tin cans from the warden's house and eked out a meal that way. It rained in the night

CHAPTER 16

and Gul (who was without the tent he'd left for the climbers at Trango) ended up in Bridgette's tent for the remainder of the night. He woke exhausted.

I woke energized and steamed out of camp at an unwise pace on our last leg of the journey. Only two miles out my energy drained and I suffered the remainder of the day. Bridgette's blisters were so bad that she borrowed Gul's socks and sandals for the 14-mile hike, but in characteristic fashion, she never complained.

As we passed the brilliant spring-green wheat fields and somber stone walls of Askole, Bridgette said she'd like to find a jeep for Skardu that night. She was desperate for a proper shower and shampoo! I groaned audibly at the thought of an arduous six- or seven-hour jeep ride on top of an eight-hour trek. Fortunately, Gul felt as I did and we collapsed into chairs at the climber's camp and imbibed Cokes, a rare luxury. Our 120-mile circuit of the Baltoro was done. So pleased was I to have finished this demanding outing that I was lulled into thinking the rest would be a cruise. I'd read and heard about the infamous Karakorum Highway, but how hard could it be to sit back and be driven for two days? Little did I know the most dangerous part of the whole journey was about to begin.

A look at the showers and I realized why Bridgette wanted to move on. They were filthy, much worse than the grey shower stalls at Jhula or Paiyu and I settled for the 'insta-shower' — four pre-moistened towelettes. It rained all night and I slept like the dead.

The jeep was leaving! I'd overslept and had to scramble. It was hard to believe how much recovery time I needed. With an afternoon nap plus regular sleep, I'd been unconscious for thirteen hours.

Thankfully our driver for the Askole-Skardu leg was more cautious than the previous driver. We learned by satellite phone that Armin and Ingvar had set up high camp on Trango, but they were back in base camp waiting out a spell of bad weather.

Following the wild crossing that separates Askole from the Shigar Valley, we stopped at a military outpost to show passports. A seemingly friendly man out of uniform asked Bridgette and I a lot of personal questions that turned a bit sinister. He wanted to see my camera to make sure there were no pictures of military buildings or bridges. It was the first time I'd heard of this injunction and I had plenty of both. I refused to give up my camera but previewed a few of the recent, less incriminating pictures. Gul returned with our passports just in time.

The Shigar Valley with its many villages has one road to connect them. Everyone and everything uses it—boys and girls in school uniforms, farmers with hoes, road workers with shovels, women carrying huge loads of wood or wheat, herds of goats, cows, donkeys, chickens. All to a fault were utterly nonchalant about our two-ton vehicle hurtling past at 30–40 mph with only inches of clearance.

We rolled into Skardu and took up residence in the Concordia Hotel once again. The shock of civilization had me feeling disoriented. Borrowing Bridgette's phone, I called Julie back in the States. The GPS locator beacon that was to inform our friends and relatives of our daily progress had worked in Europe but failed in the States. Julie had been in the dark about our whereabouts or welfare for two weeks.

From the vantage of the hotel's flat rooftop, the Indus River was looking even wilder than before and my estimate of 100,000 cubic feet per second was probably low. A little research shows that 250,000 is a better low-flood estimate for the Indus and it can go as high as 800,000 in an extreme event. Its annual output is equal to the Nile River and three times that of the Tigris-Euphrates. My previous baseline for comparison was the Colorado River. In the spring of 1983, a huge snowpack and rapid spring melt resulted in record flood levels that nearly caused the failure

Chapter 16

of Glen Canyon Dam, yet high flow was estimated at *only* 110,000 cubic feet per second.

Our driver was dressed in immaculate white traditional pants and shalwar. He was quiet, handsome, intense. Instead of a jeep, the man's own 2016 Toyota Celica was to transport us.

"Gul, how is this car going to make it over all the rough roads ahead?"

"You'll see, a jeep would be too slow for the distance we have to travel."

The driver crammed an impressive amount of gear into the small trunk while Bridgette and I had to keep our rucksacks on our laps. Our departure was a casual 9 AM, with only a six to seven-hour drive to Gilgit. The following day could easily be twice that. I took a farewell video of the bustling main street of Skardu with men, cars, and cows predominating.

We passed an agricultural plain outside of town then began a puzzling ascent. I was momentarily disoriented—rivers don't run uphill. But the road must breach the mighty Himalayan wall, just as the Indus had forced its way through the greatest range in the world. With the brief ascent over, we followed the flow of the great river, the road was a narrow slit carved out of the rock wall with many rocky overhangs. At every stream or creek confluence without culverts, water had destroyed the pavement and we crawled over rocky debris, the driver mindful of his car's undercarriage. When the road improved, we often reached freeway speed.

To my left, the rampaging Indus mesmerized me with its huge, brown rolling rapids. The stone-walled road barrier was sometimes broken or missing altogether, but nothing affected our car's speed except stream crossings and traffic. Of the latter there were heavy transport lorries lovingly painted in rainbow colors and adorned with religious symbols, like the crescent moon and star. These lorries seemed to take up the entire width of the road, but somehow our driver would badger and cajole his way around these obstacles without delay or patience. Only once did another car pass us, as it did we were taunted by a stenciled message across the back window:

THIS TOO SHALL PASS

Groups of women and children were drying apricots while boys and young men solicited the fruit roadside. Gul stopped to buy a bag. They were small, with an off-putting taste despite their international reputation.

The driver popped a cassette of traditional Pakistani music into the tape deck. It featured beguiling women vocalists, surprisingly beautiful and haunting. A small village, perhaps the equivalent of a truck stop, hosted our lunch. Even here American junk food influence had weaseled its way into this remote corner of the world, with storefront displays advertising Lay's potato chips, Coke and Pepsi.

I wished there were days not hours to spend here in the Indus River gorge. Across the river, on the occasional flat terrace, perched little villages and green fields. The wilder, less inhabited sections often had paths that led to caves or a hermit's hut. In the distance we saw the great snowy peak of Haramosh, 24,000 feet above sea level.

The canyon finally ended, we crossed a busy bridge one car at a time and then made a shocking transition to the multi-lane Karakoram Highway, (often abbreviated KKH), as smooth as an LA freeway. Here the Indus and Gilgit Rivers meet, as do three of the greatest mountain ranges in the world—the Karakoram, the Himalaya, and Hindu Kush. A half-hour detour took us to Gilgit, a huge sprawling city among fertile agricultural fields. Our dingy hotel had an indoor central courtyard with two tall, water-stressed monkey puzzle trees, leaves turning brown. My room had a large noisy air conditioner that I would run all night. By now I understood the imminently practical and water-saving

Chapter 16

shower technique of the locals. A large bucket, a small cup, and soap were the props. Fill the large bucket from the tap with water, then get wet using the cup to splash yourself. Soap up, then rinse off the same way. Voila, a complete clean using only 2 gallons of water.

At 6 PM Gul, Bridgette, and I took a taxi to see downtown Gilgit and its 700-year old mosque. Bridgette found some brand-new shoes for 500 rupees (five dollars), then the taxi driver who had been shadowing us, took us to a Chinese restaurant. No Chinese people were cooking or serving, but the décor looked authentic and the food was surprisingly good. On the wall was a full-color photograph of hikers topping the Gondogoro La. Having sent the driver away, we walked home down darkened streets, avoiding potholes and open ditches. This day was easy—tomorrow would be another story.

Bridgette and I met in the dining room at 4 AM where she woke a sleeping man in the kitchen who made us some tea and scones. The city was quiet. Outside the plate glass windows of the restaurant, we saw a shepherd with goats on the deserted street. A pack of four wild dogs harassed the herd and one or two goats actually fell in their eagerness to get away from the threat. Dogs, like in many parts of the world, are not held in particularly high esteem here.

Gul stumbled down the hall after another poor night of sleep. He'd been getting late-night calls to help organize a rescue on Nanga Parbat where climbers had been missing four days now. Our driver was a half-hour late but, having dropped off a large satchel of supplies, Bridgette and I could now fit our rucksacks into the trunk. On the edge of town, we stopped for gas. When the tank was nearly full the Toyota's back end began to bounce up and down. When I looked around the driver was producing this effect with one hand while the other was on the gas nozzle. Squeezing in every last drop. Breakfast was promised some two hours hence.

No Mere Pastime

We quickly retraced the half-hour detour of yesterday and saw a sign:

> Look to Your Left
> Killer Mountain
> Nanga Parbat 26,660 ft.

Nanga Parbat, the Naked Mountain, is the ninth highest in the world. It was invisible due to dense cloud cover. Armin and Ingvar must still have been waiting out the weather at Trango base. They were going to need some luck to succeed. Inclement weather would be this season's story and no successful climbs of K2 were to be made in 2017.

The owners were still sleeping at a roadside diner when we arrived at 7 AM, and campers out front were just rolling up their sleeping bags. Chickens destined for the cook pot scratched for seeds under scraggly eucalyptus trees. Pakistanis love chicken. This country mass produces them in factories, 95% of them transported live to markets. Lorries are often used for transport elsewhere, but here in the mountains we saw small pickup trucks being used for transporting the broilers, modified with a super-structure of interlocking cages, about the size of a large camper shell.

Our meal was a paltry single fried egg with chapatti and tea. I ordered another egg then another until I was full. The others were amused by my early morning appetite. The walls of the diner were decorated with posters of Karakoram peaks and a roster of the world's hundred highest peaks, many within a day's drive of here.

We left the KKH at Chilas for an older road over the Babusar Pass, according to our driver, a better, faster road at this time. Yet, even this road often had one lane closed due to massive boulders and gravel that had fallen from the steep hillsides. Apparently, earthmoving equipment was either in short supply or

Chapter 16

the demand was just too high. Our climb turned to steep, regular, unrelenting switchbacks, as we got stuck behind a slow-moving truck belching coal-black smoke. I pulled out a bandana to cover my face as a cheap air filter. At this elevation, the Toyota had insufficient power to pass. Men sat on the road railings and watched passing traffic while young boys sold bags of fruit. These itinerant workers lived in summer-only encampments doing what they could to survive, herding goats and sheep, growing vegetables, and selling wares and produce in fruit stands.

Babusar Pass is over 14,000 feet but here was a small village of retail stands, and Pakistani tourists milled around in sandals on the wet and muddy road. Gul said an official wanted to talk to me. *Holy shit, this is it,* I thought. This is where I get detained in some single-celled hovel of a jail, paying for the sins of Washington politicians. We tracked up a muddy hillside and entered a tent. A man attended a fire and cook pot from which unfamiliar but pleasant aromas emanated. It was dark inside but warm and I was directed to sit on a floor mattress with rough woolen blankets.

I handed my passport over to a large, impassive man who spoke to Gul in Urdu. I feared the smudge mark and exit date of my visa, altered by the Los Angeles consulate would look like my doing. I told him my name and country of origin and then he asked about my work. I am a viticulturist, a wine grape grower. The man spoke fairly good English but didn't know these words. I paused, afraid. He stared at me and I glanced at Gul who gave no help.

Then some spark prompted me to say, *"farmer"*.

The man's grave countenance broke into a wide smile. He then extended both hands to me in a ritual gesture. I didn't understand at first, then extended my hand and put it between his two. He closed his hands over mine. The beauty and sincerity of the gesture made me smile too. Suddenly, all the tension was gone and we were good to go.

The rest of the day would be one long, *long* descent to the plains and Islamabad. Like the Skardu-Gilgit road, the pavement was good, except at river crossings where it was invariably washed out. Our driver had to avoid boulders, gravel, potholes, and traffic three or four cars wide. The awful heatwave was sending people fleeing into the mountains. We saw whole families wading and swimming in the side creeks, sitting in chairs or lounges, and eating their picnic lunches. At one of these stream crossings, a clever retailer had carved out shelves in a snowbank, simultaneously displaying soft drinks for sale and keeping them ice cold.

We were off the main tourist track for foreigners for sure and Bridgette and I were the only white people in a sea of brown faces. We occasionally received curious stares but it never felt hostile. We stopped for lunch at a famous resort town called Naran where the food was plentiful and delicious, and they even found a ginger beer for me. A real beer was not possible because alcohol in a Muslim country is very difficult to find, officially forbidden. This would be our last meal of the day, but we wrapped up meat and fried potatoes in a chapatti to eat later.

Half the day was over but the second half was going to get gnarly. Worsening roads coupled with increasing traffic only spurred our driver into hyper mode. Every car ahead of us was a personal challenge to pass. His method was to pull up to within inches of the bumper, blare the horn without remorse or constraint, and whip around when they veered even slightly left (here they drive on the left-hand side). Our driver was a visionary because he could see a third, center, lane where only two existed. He would pass on blind curves and jockey for position left, right, or center, wherever was best to facilitate passing. The horn was a weapon in his hands, a weapon of intimidation, and we heard it used a thousand times that day.

Several near-collisions were avoided by our driver's incred-

Chapter 16

ible reflexes—although initially caused by his own aggressiveness. Gul joked about the movie *Fast and Furious* and said our driver could have starred in it. I was thinking it would be a miracle if we avoided some kind of calamity. Our driver would mutter to himself when a car didn't move over fast enough for his liking. Once he brought the car to a quick stop, opened the door, leaned out, and gave the evil eye to the driver of a receding car who did not stand down to his intimidation.

In a narrow gorge, the traffic suddenly slowed down and cars merged into five or six unorderly lines, then stopped. We heard rumors of a landslide ahead. I welcomed the chance to stretch my legs but came back without a report. Gul reproached me for going out alone and said it could have been dangerous in this crowd. Later the driver, Gul, and I walked down together. Bridgette, guilty only of being a woman, had to stay in the locked car. She was suffering from blisters, then a cold, followed by a bad hacking cough, and now as a virtual prisoner, she was still smiling and accepting of the situation.

An excavator machine had fallen into the river a hundred feet below the highway. No word on whether anyone was inside at the time. A large crane was trying to retrieve it. When we returned, Bridgette had made friends with three Muslim women in the next vehicle over. They loved the fact she was wearing traditional Pakistani garb. We had an excruciating two-hour delay before we moved again, with the excavator still in the river. The Indy 500 began immediately and soon I was feeling ill. Carsickness was novel to me. The heat and humidity, the constant stop and go, and the insane antics of the driver had done me in. Gul noticed and we exchanged seats—I felt better in the back seat where it was a little cooler and a tad farther from the action.

I'll admit our driver was a talented multi-tasker: he could talk on his cell phone, converse with Gul, and drive one-handed, zipping around dozens of cars, all while daring the gorge's deep drop-offs. It reminds me of a quote from Robert

No Mere Pastime

Louis Stevenson's *Silverado Squatters* about Clark Foss, the most famous stagecoach driver in the West at that time:

> *California boasts her famous stage-drivers, and among the famous Foss is not forgotten. Along the unfenced, abominable mountain roads he launches his team with small regard to human life or the doctrine of probabilities. Flinching travelers, who behold themselves coasting eternity at every corner, look with natural admiration at the driver's huge, impassive, fleshy countenance... Wonderful tales are current of his readiness and skill. One in particular of how one of his horses fell at a ticklish passage of the road, and how Foss let slip the reins, and driving over the fallen animal, arrived at the next stage with only three.*

That day, I was hoping not to lose any horses.

Late afternoon found us in a nightmarish traffic jam in the city of Abbottabad. Every few feet the driver stomped on the brakes, pulled the parking brake (on level ground), and fumed. When a few feet of space opened, he released the parking brake, screeched ahead, slammed on the brakes, and set the parking brake again. This went on for nearly an hour. Only on my return home did I remember that Abbottabad was the final hangout of Osama bin Laden.

In the foothills at dusk, some city folks were camped for the night and erecting tents or sleeping in cars. Cook fires were common. You could tell city folk from country by their Westernized clothing. The possession of a cell phone was no indication of class or status. Everyone down to the poorest peasant in a country shack had at least a cheap Chinese model. Mobile phone outlets were commonplace—we saw the largest in the country, Jazz Cash, advertised everywhere.

Dusk was upon us as we left the foothills and hit the plains. There was no slowing down except when the superhighway suddenly and without warning turned to gravel. Oncoming car

Chapter 16

lights were often fixed on high-beam. You'd see entire families on a single motorcycle, husband driving, wife sidesaddle, brother in the back, little sister riding on the handlebars, almost always without helmets. Often, open lorries carrying a dozen or so people in the back had several of the men balanced on the back bumper while keeping up with the flow of traffic. The air was opaque, impenetrable, full of powerful odors like diesel exhaust fumes and rotting carcasses. Miles of food stand concessions lined the highway and people dined close to the brawling traffic.

I know this was nothing unusual for the locals, even for millions of people around the world. I may even, given enough time, have come to think of it as normal. But after 15 hours in a moving target I was overwhelmed with sensory overload and went inside myself, looking for a respite in the eye of this storm.

The driver pulled over during a deserted section of highway to wash his dirty windshield. Out of nowhere a man and a young girl walked by. He was holding her hand, but her face was full of anxiety and fright. I feared for her. What in the world were they doing?

The relief was palpable when for a short stretch the windows were rolled up and the air conditioner came on. But soon the A/C was off, the windows went down and the chaos and cacophony of the highway resumed. Finally, we arrived in Islamabad, sixteen hours from Gilgit, and at the hotel was an escape from the maelstrom. The room was quiet, immaculate, cavernous, with a king bed and TV, even slippers for the shower, a western one. I ate the last of the fried potatoes from lunch and fell into fathomless unconsciousness.

In contrast to my shocking introduction to Islamabad, the following day my experience would turn 180 degrees. Vendors plied wares outside my window in the hazy sunshine. The hotel had no restaurant but room service was standard there. They brought me breakfast and lunch while I rested and wrote in my journal.

In the afternoon Gul, Bridgette, and I visited the largest mosque in Pakistan, named for King Faisal of Saudi Arabia. Its contemporary design was inspired by the iconic form of a Bedouin tent and was flanked by four soaring minarets, each 260 feet tall. Walking in with hundreds of other people we had to leave our bags and shoes behind. Acres of white stone were hot and burnt my tender bare feet. The main worship hall, full of cushions but no chairs, can accommodate 100,000 people, while in the courtyard up to 200,000 for special events. Today there were perhaps five or ten thousand, many ignoring the prominent signs that prohibited photography and cautioned parents to keep children close by and quiet.

Family of four on motorcycle, Islamabad, Pakistan

Chapter

Twice we were greeted warmly by strangers. They asked us if we were enjoying our stay in Pakistan. A group of young men invited me to have a group photo taken with them. We shook hands but also placed hands on hearts to bid goodbye. I couldn't imagine anything like this happening to foreigners in the United States. I was amazed and touched by this spontaneous generosity.

We drove to the highest hilltop in the city for drinks at an Italian restaurant. From here we could look down on this well-planned city that sprang full-blown from the desert in the early 1960s, its location was chosen due to the convergence of two major rivers, the Indus and the Attaq. It is divided into 12 distinct sectors. Some say it is a cold and sterile design. But from up here the overall effect was green with many plantings of trees. I was glad to have this second view of Islamabad on my last full day in Pakistan. There was good news from Armin via the satellite phone—he and Ingvar topped the Great Trango yesterday in a weather window they had waited for patiently. Ingvar became the first person from Sweden to summit the Great Trango.

"Excuse me, sir," came the ever so polite voice, "it's 2:30 AM."

Groggy with only 3 ½ hours of sleep, I left the oasis of my air-conditioned room and hit a wall of humidity and heat in the hallway. It must have been 95° F. A useless fan whirled at the reception desk and suddenly I felt horrible. I was tempted to lie down on a couch had an employee not already been sleeping there. Gul and Bridgette were twenty minutes late and when the taxi arrived I sat like a zombie. All of us were too wiped out for much conversation. At the airport, we said our final goodbyes and while waiting in line my sickness slowly receded.

Turkish Airlines supercooled their planes and I was not the only one to wrap up in the blanket provided to ward off the chill. After a meal, the plane was darkened and people slept, many with the blanket covering their head.

My journey had been the most intense, and at the same time, the truest of my life. Nearly every day for a month I had been stretched up to and beyond my limits. Suddenly, tears were falling down my face and I wept silently. I wept over all the imaginary fears that never materialized and for pure exhaustion. They were tears of relief, tears of joy and gratitude for all the wonderful people I had met, the common folk who, the world over, are decent and wish for nothing but peace for themselves and others. I was grateful that somehow I was able to keep moving and accomplish a life-long goal. In the process I gained far more than I sought. I felt completely broken open by emotion.

I hoped my flights home would be smooth and eventless but that would be inconsistent with the rest of the trip, would it not? At London's Heathrow airport my connecting flight was late and I had only 15 minutes to sprint across the length of the second busiest international airport in the world, an airport I'd never been to. The ten-hour flight back home was a picnic compared to the KKH but one last glitch awaited. My Patagonia duffel didn't make it out of London with me and it was three days before it arrived at my doorstep.

That duffel, lashed by woven rope to the side of a mule for two weeks over the most inhospitable terrain, arrived at camp intact and unharmed every day. If I had to choose who I trust more, an international airline or a porter and his mule, I believe the Balti will win that contest.

Perched boulder on ice pillar, Baltoro Glacier, Karakoram Himalaya

Gasherbrum IV from Concordia, Karakoram, Pakistan

K2 with cloud cap, from Concordia, Karakoram, Pakistan

Uli Biaho mountains reflected in lake, Great Trango Base Camp, Karakoram

*Mule carrying duffels,
Baltoro Glacier, Karakoram*

About the Author

Ken Stanton was born, raised and educated in Los Angeles, playing competitive sports from an early age and was briefly ranked in the junior category with the United States Lawn Tennis Association. Ken graduated with a Bachelor of Arts degree from the University of California at Santa Barbara in 1975. By then he had found his life's passion in mountaineering, pursuing most aspects of the sport including bouldering, cragging, canyoneering, big wall climbing and alpine climbing in the Western United States, Canada, and Europe. Ken is a co-owner of Stanton Vineyards Inc., based in Napa Valley, where his family grows seven varieties of premium red wine grapes. His most rewarding work has been authorship and publication of three successful books and numerous articles in newspapers, periodicals and magazines. *Mt St Helena and RLS State Park: a history and guide* was published in 1993. *Great Day Hikes in and Around Napa Valley* published in 1995 and was reviewed in the *New York Times* in 2007. The author co-wrote *Napa Valley Picnic* with Jack Burton, in 2001. Stanton lives in the small college town of Angwin with his life partner Julie Lazar, a recognized contemporary art curator.

ABOOKS

ALIVE Book Publishing and ALIVE Publishing Group
are imprints of Advanced Publishing LLC,
3200 A Danville Blvd., Suite 204, Alamo, California 94507

Telephone: 925.837.7303
alivebookpublishing.com

www.ingramcontent.com/pod-product-compliance
Lightning Source LLC
Chambersburg PA
CBHW040902250426

43672CB00034B/2984